Here's Health

HEALTHY
DESSERTS

Here's Health

HEALTHY DESSERTS

Janette Marshall

HAMLYN

Published 1985 by Hamlyn Publishing,
a division of The Hamlyn Publishing Group Ltd,
Bridge House, London Road, Twickenham, Middlesex

ISBN 0 600 32486 9

Illustrations by Elaine Hill
Photography by Chris Crofton

Filmset in Linotron Goudy by Wyvern Typesetting Limited, Bristol
Printed in Spain

Endpapers: *Israeli Fruit Salad (page 38),
Apricot and Lemon Cream (page 56), Crepes Suzette (page 89)*

Previous page: *Pistachio Ice Cream (page 69),
Chestnut Choux Rings (page 92), Lime and Kiwi Terrine (page 84)*

Contents

Useful Facts and Figures

Notes on metrication

In this book quantities are given in metric and Imperial measures. Exact conversion from Imperial to metric measures does not usually give very convenient working quantities and so the metric measures have been rounded off into units of 25 grams. The table below shows the recommended equivalents.

Ounces	Approx g to nearest whole figure	Recommended conversion to nearest unit of 25	Ounces	Approx g to nearest whole figure	Recommended conversion to nearest unit of 25
1	28	25	11	312	300
2	57	50	12	340	350
3	85	75	13	368	375
4	113	100	14	396	400
5	142	150	15	425	425
6	170	175	16 (1 lb)	454	450
7	198	200	17	482	475
8	227	225	18	510	500
9	255	250	19	539	550
10	283	275	20 (1¼ lb)	567	575

Note: When converting quantities over 20 oz first add the appropriate figures in the centre column, then adjust to the nearest unit of 25. As a general guide, 1 kg (1000 g) equals 2·2 lb or about 2 lb 3 oz. This method of conversion gives good results in nearly all cases, although in certain pastry and cake recipes a more accurate conversion is necessary to produce a balanced recipe.

Liquid measures The millilitre has been used in this book and the following table gives a few examples.

Imperial	Approx ml to nearest whole figure	Recommended ml	Imperial	Approx ml to nearest whole figure	Recommended ml
¼ pint	142	150 ml	1 pint	567	600 ml
½ pint	283	300 ml	1½ pints	851	900 ml
¾ pint	425	450 ml	1¾ pints	992	1000 ml (1 litre)

Spoon measures All spoon measures given in this book are level unless otherwise stated.
Can sizes At present, cans are marked with the exact (usually to the nearest whole number) metric equivalent of the Imperial weight of the contents, so we have followed this practice when giving can sizes.

Oven temperatures

The table below gives recommended equivalents.

	°C	°F	Gas Mark
Very cool	110	225	$\frac{1}{4}$
	120	250	$\frac{1}{2}$
Cool	140	275	1
	150	300	2
Moderate	160	325	3
	180	350	4
Moderately hot	190	375	5
	200	400	6
Hot	220	425	7
	230	450	8
Very hot	240	475	9

Notes for American and Australian users

In America the 8-fl oz measuring cup is used. In Australia metric measures are now used in conjunction with the standard 250-ml measuring cup. The Imperial pint, used in Britain and Australia, is 20 fl oz, while the American pint is 16 fl oz. It is important to remember that the Australian tablespoon differs from both the British and American tablespoons; the table below gives a comparison. The British standard tablespoon, which has been used throughout this book, holds 17·7 ml, the American 14·2 ml, and the Australian 20 ml. A teaspoon holds approximately 5 ml in all three countries.

British	American	Australian
1 teaspoon	1 teaspoon	1 teaspoon
1 tablespoon	1 tablespoon	1 tablespoon
2 tablespoons	3 tablespoons	2 tablespoons
$3\frac{1}{2}$ tablespoons	4 tablespoons	3 tablespoons
4 tablespoons	5 tablespoons	$3\frac{1}{2}$ tablespoons

An Imperial/American guide to solid and liquid measures

Imperial	American	Imperial	American
Solid measures		*Liquid measures*	
1 lb butter or margarine	2 cups	$\frac{1}{4}$ pint liquid	$\frac{2}{3}$ cup liquid
1 lb flour	4 cups	$\frac{1}{2}$ pint	$1\frac{1}{4}$ cups
1 lb granulated or caster sugar	2 cups	$\frac{3}{4}$ pint	2 cups
1 lb icing sugar	3 cups	1 pint	$2\frac{1}{2}$ cups
8 oz rice	1 cup	$1\frac{1}{2}$ pints	$3\frac{3}{4}$ cups
		2 pints	5 cups ($2\frac{1}{2}$ pints)

Note: When making any of the recipes in this book, only follow one set of measures as they are not interchangeable.

Introduction

'Healthy Desserts' may seem like a contradiction in terms. Indeed this book does not set out to argue the case for desserts, but it does intend to to show that it is possible for desserts to make a valuable, nutritional contribution to a meal.

If that sounds boring and stodgy (like some health or wholefood restaurant desserts) then do read on because the recipes in this book are from another school of thought. They show that by using various easy techniques, and by making the most of the versatility of fresh fruits and other natural foods, you can make exciting desserts that are light and attractive as well as being delicious and wholesome.

This book contains featherlight, pretty desserts that are low in fat, sugar, butter and eggs. (Cream is completely excluded from the recipes.) That is because these ingredients have recently acquired 'health risk' status in the quantities in which they are eaten in the typical Western diet. Desserts, puddings, cakes and biscuits are often the vehicles that put the excess fat and sugar into our mouths: so by changing the ingredients in desserts you can re-educate your taste away from sugary, fatty food.

Some of the recipes will be naturally high in fibre because of their fruit content, but with a sensible diet (see page 28) other elements of the day's eating can provide sufficient roughage so there is no need for heavy wholemeal desserts using lots of flour, grains, cereals and dried fruits. Instead desserts can provide more of the vitamins and minerals that are needed in our diet from the fresh ingredients.

Healthy Desserts will be useful when you are entertaining – because on these occasions a dessert or pudding course is virtually obligatory. These recipes, however, will not leave your guests feeling slightly sickly and sugary or wishing that they had not indulged! However not all the recipes are for special occasions: there are also simple dishes for home and family use when you feel like a delicious dessert.

How can desserts be healthy?

'Healthy' desserts mean different things to different people. At one time milk puddings and nursery foods such as roly poly, Spotted Dick and suet treacle puddings were considered good, especially for children, because they were based on milk and sugar – both thought to be excellent foods.

As more facts have come to light, the trend of thought has changed since the days when nanny ruled in the nursery. Those nursery children have also changed – into adults who have weight and health problems which are directly related to what we eat.

There have been several government reports on food and health in the last few decades. The best known of the more recent reports on the subject is that by the National Advisory Committee on Nutrition Education (NACNE). Their controversial findings caused a stir in July 1983 because the conclusion was, in brief, that the typical British (or Western) diet was actually making us ill. The report stated that too much fat, sugar and salt are consumed and not enough natural, unprocessed, high-fibre foods (which also provide valuable nutrients such as vitamins and minerals) are being eaten. The very elements that are of most value to us in our food are being removed by modern methods of processing.

The Committee on the Medical Aspects of Food Policy (COMA) report of July 1984, which investigated diet in relation to heart disease, reinforced the findings of NACNE. This is important when thinking about desserts because fat (butter, margarine, suet, lard, chocolate, eggs, milk and the different types of cream) and sugar (from icing sugar to raw cane sugar, plus fondants, etc.) are the main ingredients in most desserts.

So *Healthy Desserts* gives you ways of making light and attractive desserts using as little fat and sugar as possible. It also provides an alternative to the wholemeal desserts that have (until recently with the advent of the healthier *nouvelle cuisine*) been the only 'healthy' desserts available. Although high in fibre from ingredients such as wholemeal flour, rolled oats, bran and wheatgerm, dried fruits and nuts, many wholemeal desserts are also high in fat and sugar. There existed the erroneous belief that somehow brown sugar was all right but in fact all sugar is equally bad and the minute amount of minerals carried in raw cane sugar is not enough to make a nutritional contribution to the diet.

People are gradually becoming more discriminating and are not prepared to put up with mass-produced offerings either, such as the ubiquitous Black Forest Gâteau or cheesecake. There is, after all, something better, and here it is . . .

What's so special about these desserts?

It has been mentioned previously how the new approach to cooking has placed greater emphasis on lightness, presentation and colour. All of which you might think is not new. Indeed there is lightness in a meringue, attractiveness and colour in a well-decorated gâteau and a combination of all three in pavlovas, ice-cream bombes etc. But the difference here is that the criteria has been achieved using a different set of ingredients – healthy ones.

That means that cream is not included and the use of other sources of fat like butter, margarine, egg yolks and oils are minimised. Regular sugar is abandoned and the use of flour is kept down and when it is used wholemeal replaces the ordinary white flour. Yet these desserts are still pleasing to the eye as much as to the palate and because they do not use a lot of fat and sugar they provide a more easily digestible dessert.

By employing methods that trap air such as the whisked sponge, desserts can be made that are as light as a feather, even though they are made of wholemeal flour and therefore have a good fibre content. They will also be lower in calories than regular desserts because they are made without fat.

Air can also be incorporated into desserts by whisking egg whites to stiff peaks and then folding them in to mixtures such as fruit purées to make mousses and soufflés, foam sauces, whips and creams. Setting agents like gelatine and agar agar can then be added to trap the air and hold the mixture in suspension, preventing it from collapsing.

Shortcrust pastry is not used in these recipes because of its high fat content. Other pastries such as flaky, puff and rough puff pastry are similarly excluded as they contain even more fat than shortcrust. However there are some 'pastries' which use a lot less fat and choux pastry, for example, is good because it produces a light airy result that is low in fat.

Yeast will also act as a raising agent and again avoids the need for fats like butter that trap air in puff pastries to make them rise. Yeasted pastries, provided they are low in fat, are also lower in calories. Wholemeal flour can be successfully used in these recipes to give a higher fibre content and they make super rum babas and other savarin desserts. Syrups can be made with fruit juices and spices to replace the usual sugary syrups.

Salt-based raising agents such as bicarbonate of soda and baking powder can also be avoided by using whisked sponge and yeast methods.

These desserts are also made special by the things that go into them as well as the ingredients that are left out. Many of them

may be new to you so here is a useful glossary to explain some of the ingredients that you might be encountering for the first time in these recipes.

Agar-agar

This is the vegetarian equivalent of gelatine which can be used for setting mousses, soufflés and some cheesecakes. It is also known under the name of agar on its own or Japanese isinglass. Agar-agar is a naturally occurring derivative of seaweed which is available from health food shops in powder form or as flakes (that look like little soap flakes). For instructions for use see page 29.

Butter (see also Fats)

Unsalted butter is used throughout this book because it does not contain salt or colouring.

Carob

This is a chocolate substitute that is available in bars or in powder form (the latter is sometimes called carob flour and is used in place of cocoa powder or drinking chocolate). The advantages of carob are that it is naturally sweeter than cocoa so carob products need less sugar adding than chocolate. Carob also contains more calcium than chocolate, less oxalic acid – making it less likely to cause skin blemishes – and above all it is free from caffeine and theobromine, both of which are stimulants with addictive properties. Carob powder always needs sifting because it tends to be lumpier than cocoa powder. Remember to store it in a dry place.

Cassis

This blackcurrant syrup can replace sugar as a sweetener in some fruit dishes and sauces. Although it is made with sugar it does mean that less is used overall and that it is used in a more imaginative way with the added flavour

of the fruit. Cassis is made in France from blackcurrants and the brand called Monin is made without colouring and contains only concentrated blackcurrant juice and natural fruit extracts together with sugar.

Cheese

The cheeses used in these desserts are low-calorie ones such as cottage, ricotta, quark and low-fat curd cheese. They can make very successful cheesecakes, moulded desserts and mousse-style puddings – just as good as full-fat cream cheese. The low-fat soft white cheeses like quark do have more whey (liquid) so it is best to use a setting agent with them in some cases, especially in cheesecakes to avoid soggy bases. The other advantage of these cheeses is that they are lighter in texture and less cloying than cream cheeses. Semi-soft goats' milk cheese is used in some recipes as it has a really excellent flavour when it is combined with fruit.

Most commercially made cottage cheeses contain preservatives and stabilisers, but some made by small dairies are free from these additives. These can usually be bought in good health and wholefood shops, in speciality cheese shops and delicatessens.

Coffee

Wherever a recipe calls for coffee flavouring decaffeinated coffee has been specified. This can be bought as instant granules, as ready-ground coffee or as decaffeinated beans. The removal of the caffeine means that you can enjoy the flavour of coffee without its addictive or stimulant properties, or other possible side effects.

Eggs

Free-range eggs are now becoming more widely available – even supermarkets are beginning to stock them. I use them because of humanitarian reasons and also because the

chickens are less likely to be fed antibiotics as part of their food – or to be subjected to other drugs – because their living conditions keep them healthier. The result of this is that there is less likelihood of residues of these additives in the eggs. Some battery egg producers actually add artificial colouring to the hens' food to dye the yolks a deep and uniform yellow to mimic that of naturally 'healthy' eggs.

Essences

Although all the recipes in this book avoid any form of artificial or chemical colouring or additives some natural essences are useful, especially natural vanilla essence and natural bitter almond essence. Look for the word 'essence' on the bottle label and avoid those marked 'flavouring' as they contain a synthetically made, imitation flavour. It is also useful to have natural oils such as orange or lemon available sometimes. If you have problems in obtaining these they can be bought by post from Culpeper Ltd, 21 Bruton Street, London W1.

Fats

Although these recipes are low in fat for health reasons we cannot shun the butter versus margarine debate. This centres around the saturated fats contained in butter and the polyunsaturated content of some, but not all, soft vegetable margarines. Cholesterol is normally contained in all animal tissue so anything of animal origin – such as butter – may be a source of it in our diet. Whereas dairy produce is rich in cholesterol, vegetable fats contain none. As a high blood cholesterol level has been linked with heart disease the government has recommended that the quantity of saturated fat eaten be reduced to 15 per cent of our total fat intake and that in turn should be no more than 35 per cent of our total food intake. A lot of health experts would like to see us eat even less fat but we do need to eat some because there are two fatty acids (linoleic and linolenic) which are essential for health and which we cannot manufacture in the body.

To sum up, generally cut down on the

amount of fat eaten and used in cooking and make sure that most of what you do eat is high in polyunsaturates.

Flour (see also Thickeners)

There is not a lot of flour used in *Healthy Desserts* because we are aiming for a lighter style of dessert, but the flour that is used is 100 per cent wholemeal, unless it is stated that it is 85 per cent in the recipe. The label 100 per cent wholemeal means that it is the whole grain of wheat which has been ground into flour and none of the bran or wheatgerm has been extracted as it has in white flour. This means the flour contains all its dietary fibre and the valuable B vitamins and vitamin E which are lost in the milling of white flour. The whisked sponge method, used in the gâteaux section in particular, will show you how lighter-than air desserts are possible with wholemeal flour. I use 85 per cent extraction flour for choux pastry because it is unsuccessful with 100 per cent. Some of the crepes in the book are made using buckwheat flour. This is a natural buckwheat grain which is ground, like wholemeal flour, using the whole grain so it is high in vitamins and fibre. It has a greyer colour than wholemeal flour and does not have a high gluten content which gives wheat flours their natural elasticity to make bread and cakes rise, so buckwheat flour cannot be used in general baking.

Fruit

Fresh fruit on its own is probably the finest dessert of all. It is recommended that you buy organically-grown fruit because it is produced without the use of chemical fertilisers, sprays or other chemicals used to regulate pest control or even help the fruit turn the right colour at the right time for the farmer. Residues of these chemicals are bound to find their way into the fruit which we consume and there is concern about the effect (espe-cially the long-term, unknown effects) these might have on health. Organically-grown produce is not yet easily available but demand is making it more so and a lot is now being imported from Europe where organic food is more widely available than in Britain. The principles of organic farming and a list of British stockists is given in *The Organic Food Guide*, edited by Alan Gear and published by Henry Doubleday Research Association.

Dried fruit gives desserts a natural sweetness (like some spices) without adding sugar. Soaking fruit overnight in natural fruit juice enhances the sweetness and is used in some of these recipes. The only really natural way to dry food is by the sun. This method evaporates the water content thus naturally concentrating the sugars in the fruit and so preserving it because there is not enough moisture left to support the bacteria which lead to decay. Other methods use alkaline emulsions on the fruit to speed the drying process. The fruit is then also coated with mineral oils to make it seem shiny and appetising, and it may be treated with sulphur dioxide to help preserve the colour (this is especially true of apricots). Do read the labels and avoid dried fruit containing preservatives and mineral oil coatings.

Canned fruit is often convenient in the winter when there is not much fresh fruit about or when it is expensive. If using canned fruit choose from the increasing number of varieties that are canned either in their own natural juice or in apple juice. These varieties are usually free from added sugar. Some slimmers' or diabetics' fruits are canned in water.

Concentrated fruit juice is a useful natural sweetener and it avoids the use of added sugar. Various varieties are available from health food shops or delicatessens but the most useful, I find, is apple juice which is also a delicious drink when diluted and flavoured with some fresh mint leaves!

Fructose

This is the name for the naturally occurring sugar in fruit which is extracted to make a sugar which looks like ordinary white granulated sugar but has slightly larger granules. It is used in small quantities in this book because it is much sweeter than sucrose (the normal sugar) and it is expensive. Fructose is also less disruptive to blood sugar levels than sucrose, which is why it is often used in diabetic foods. This disruption of blood sugar levels can lead to moodiness, craving for sweet things and hypoglycaemia (low blood sugar).

Gelatine

Gelatine, like agar-agar, is a natural setting agent or thickener which is made from ground horn and hoof (that is why vegetarians may prefer not to use it). In powder form 15 g/½ oz gelatine is the equivalent of 3 teaspoons. Gelatine may also be bought as 'leaves' which are dissolved in hot water or other liquid, but these are mainly used by professional cooks. See page 29 for instructions on use.

Gelozone

This is the brand name of a vegetable powder which describes itself as the 'vegetable alternative to gelatine'. It does not contain agar but is a mixture of guar gum (a gum extracted from a type of pea plant native to India but also grown in America), carrageenan (also called Irish moss, a natural extract of several seaweeds) and locust bean gum (an extract from the carob tree seeds). See page 29 for instructions on use.

Grenadine

In Britain the grenadine is called the pomegranate and from it is made another syrup, like cassis. I find grenadine brings out the flavour of some fruit sauces and dishes very well. It is made using sugar, but less is required than ordinary sugar and it has a flavour all of its own. It goes especially well with raspberries. Like cassis, it is available from some off-licences, delicatessens and supermarkets. Sirop de grenadine is made without colouring or additives and contains sugar, vanilla, citric acid and natural colouring from fruit juice.

Honey

Most of the gâteau recipes use clear honey rather than sugar in the sponge method. I prefer honey because of its consistency: it gives a moister sponge than sugar because it is hygroscopic (absorbing or attracting moisture from the air). I find less honey than sugar needs to be used for the same sweetness and it is also mainly fructose and glucose rather than sucrose. These former two sugars are less disruptive to blood sugar levels than sucrose, but they are still sugars and honey should be treated as such and used in moderation. It does contain vitamins and minerals which sugar does not but they are in minute amounts which are of nutritional insignificance. Slightly lower temperatures are needed when cooking with honey because it will burn more easily than sugar. Choose a light clear honey for cooking because it will be more delicate in flavour and a strong honey can spoil the taste of a gâteau.

Jam

Ordinary jam is not included in this book because it is high in sugar and in many cases contains preservatives, colourings and other additives. However the no-added sugar range of jams are extremely useful. They are set with pectin and sweetened with apple juice and are suitable for diabetics. More importantly they are delicious—like real fruit purées. Remember to refrigerate once opened because they do not keep as long as regular

jam as they do not have the high concentration of sucrose to inhibit bacterial growth.

Margarine (see also Fats)

Most people choose margarine because it offers unsaturated and polyunsaturated fatty acids (PUFAs) as opposed to the saturated kind found in butter. However not all margarines are the same because the amount of PUFAs vary.

Some soft vegetable margarines are high in polyunsaturates and the labels should disclose the percentage of PUFAs in the product. Amongst the highest in polyunsaturates are Flora, Prewett's Sunflower, Prewett's Safflower, Co-op Good Life, Kraft Sunflower, Kraft Vitalife Sunflower and Vitaquell.

Margarine does have its critics because it is made by a complicated chemical process and requires the use of food additives such as emulsifiers, colouring and antioxidants which are not used in butter. However some margarines are made from cold-pressed oils which means less processing and others are also produced from vegetable oils.

It is a myth that margarine is more 'slimming' than butter, both have virtually the same calories – it is only special 'spreads' like Outline and St Ivel's Gold which have fewer calories and that is because they have extra water added.

Milk

Because milk is high in fat, especially saturated fat, I use skimmed milk in the recipes in this book. It makes just as good baked custards and desserts. Pasteurised skimmed milk is now widely available and is preferable to UHT long-life as it has a better flavour.

Dried skimmed milk powder is also useful as a standby and can be used in many recipes. Skimmed milk has approximately 100 calories per pint compared with about 250 contained in a pint of whole pasteurised (silver-top) milk. Soya milk has about the same calorific value as skimmed milk but it contains different nutrients. Soya milk may be substituted for dairy milk by vegans and this has the same advantages because it is low

in fat and calories. Vegan yogurt can be made using soya milk and a freeze-dried sachet of yogurt culture.

Oil

Very little oil is used in the making of *Healthy Desserts* but it is worth mentioning that where oil is used for cooking choose a variety that is more stable at high temperatures, such as corn or soy oil; with a cold-pressed oil, such as sunflower or safflower, which is high in polyunsaturates, for cold use.

Tahini

Tahini is a thick paste of lightly roasted, ground sesame seeds which can be used as a natural sweetener or thickener. It is traditionally mixed with honey and ground nuts to make halva. Its creamy consistency makes it very useful as a substitute for cream in certain recipes.

Thickeners

Apart from agar-agar, Gelozone and gelatine which are used as setting agents and thickeners, potato flour and arrowroot are used to thicken sauces and some jelly-like desserts. The potato flour or arrowroot is mixed with cold water to a paste and then added to hot liquids which are returned to the heat and cooked for a couple of minutes, stirring all the time, until they thicken.

Tofu

This is widely used in Japanese and Chinese cooking where it is mainly a source of protein in savoury main courses. It is made from soya beans which are boiled and ground to make a soya milk which is then coagulated into curds in the same way as cheese, but a bacteria culture, not rennet, is used. The resultant soft curd is tofu and is high in protein and has only traces of fat and sugars. It can be used in desserts to make creamy mousses, ice-creams, whips etc. It is wonderfully versatile because it has virtually no flavour of its own and very few calories.

Yogurt

One could write a book about yogurt (and some people have). The advantage of yogurt in *Healthy Desserts* is as a substitute for cream. All types of cream are high in fats and calories and are to be avoided. Until now it has been difficult to find a yogurt with the right consistency to substitute for cream (mixtures of yogurt and soft cheeses have been the most successful) but strained Greek yogurt is the answer. This yogurt is strained after being made to drain off all the whey (liquid). The watery whey does not appear when you dip into this yogurt and this makes it suitable for use in desserts because it will not 'weep', it will hold its texture and will not make things go soggy. It can be made at home by making natural yogurt (see page 120) and simply placing it in butter muslin or thin cheesecloth and hanging it up to drain overnight. In the morning a creamy thick yogurt will be left in the muslin which can be scraped out and then kept in the refrigerator in a tub.

Junior Desserts, Sliced Fruit (page 24), Natural Yogurt with Raspberry Sauce (pages 120 & 113), Fruit Yogurt with Strawberries (page 121)

Healthy desserts for babies and children

Today's parents, with the benefit of hindsight in seeing the damage sweets, and sugar in its many other forms, has done to their generation, are trying to keep their children away from sweets. Many do it simply to save teeth (and to promote good skin in older children, because chocolate in particular is very bad for the complexion) but others do it because they recognise that taste is developed early in life and that many foods used by parents as rewards or bribery later in life become comforters (consciously or subconsciously). Food is also a question of habit for many people so it is just as well to get children into good habits early in life.

Of course babies and toddlers do not *need* dessert courses with their meals, but this is the time when the wonderful range of flavours and textures of fruit can be introduced to them; from the ubiquitous stewed apple to the exotic kiwi fruit. Fruit purées are often one of the first solid foods introduced to babies but grated and mashed raw fruits can also be taken in tiny amounts at the later stages of weaning.

As baby becomes older, yogurts, yogurt-based whips and fools, baked custards etc. can be introduced and later on slices and segments of whole fruits can be given as well as fruit with stones for the three-year-old child upwards.

However, even at the toddler stage, when the child is sharing family meals, it is best to keep them away from pastries, puddings or sponges and give them just fruit or yogurt. From as early an age as possible it is best to introduce children to family food and avoid cooking or serving special baby food because the child should enjoy good food with the rest of the family (puréed or prepared however necessary) rather than have to suffer the often aromaless commercially bottled or canned baby foods.

There is no need for a lot of special equipment for preparing desserts for babies; a good fork is really all that is required for mashing small quantities of stewed or raw fruit for small babies. However, as with all preparation up to seven months or so, all equipment for preparing baby food should be sterilised, and stringent hygiene should apply to washing and storing baby's utensils. This is not so necessary if you have a dishwasher because its high temperature will be sufficient.

For preparing slightly larger quantities a nylon sieve is useful for fruits and desserts: do

not use a metal sieve for fruit. The sieve should be washed well and rinsed with boiling water. A stainless steel potato masher might also be useful for fruits without pips and seeds. For fruits with pips and seeds a food mill is more suitable because it collects the seeds and pips on the top of the blade allowing only the pulp to pass into the collecting bowl beneath.

Large quantities, and batches for the freezer, are best made in a food processor, blender or liquidiser; but remember to sieve any pippy fruits through a nylon sieve for babies up to about eight months old.

For cooking fruit use a stainless steel or glass saucepan with a heavy base: the heavy base is so that the fruit does not burn or stick. Stainless steel or glass saucepans are preferable to aluminium because they do not react with the food. Fruit can erode minute amounts of aluminium from the surface of the saucepan (that's what makes saucepans shiny after fruit or other acidic foods have been prepared in them) which is not thought to be good for health. Stainless steel pans also give better distribution of heat, they look smarter and cleaner and last longer. Cast-irons pans are not really suitable, unless they are enamel lined, because they may also lose minute amounts of surface into the fruit, however this is not thought to be harmful like aluminium. Similarly use stainless steel knives for cutting fruit. Microwave ovens could also be used to cook fruit.

The main benefit of preparing your own desserts for babies and children is that you can leave out the sugar and spare your children the early development of a sweet tooth. Most fruits do not need any sweetening (with the exception of rhubarb and very sharp plums) and because sweetness is very much a question of taste you can ensure your children develop good taste. You can also help them avoid the barrage of chemical additives from cosmetic colourings to flavourings, preservatives, stabilisers, antioxidants and the rest. These are often present in products of the food industry aimed specifically at children. Garish colour is used to appeal to children, for example. As there are no studies on the long-term effect of food additives and, as many are under suspicion of having ill effects on health, it is best to protect young children in particular from exposure to them as far as practicable (or sociable).

An increasing volume of evidence is accumulating to suggest that food additives, especially colourings, are responsible for many cases of hyperactivity in children, allergies and even asthma and eczema – many cases of which can result in learning disabilities and put children at an early disadvantage.

Remember to try one fruit at a time because some children develop allergies to certain foods that often disappear at a later stage. It is also probably best to stick to a single fruit at one serving for the baby to get used to the different flavours, but there is no reason why you should not mix up combinations of fruits in the purées, especially to get slightly thicker purées by adding stewed apple to fruits like gooseberries.

Weaning to six months:

Stewed fruit:
apples
pears
plums

To prepare: peel and quarter then poach in a few tablespoons of water before puréeing. In the case of plums, stone and poach, then remove skins and mash or purée.

Dried fruits:
apricots
prunes
peaches
apples

To prepare: pre-soak the fruits if necessary, then cook in boiling water in stainless steel, glass or an enamel-lined cast-iron saucepan and stone when the fruit is cold enough to handle, then purée.

Raw purees:
peaches
nectarines
apricots
plums

To prepare: plunge the fruit into boiling water then into cold for 2 minutes to facilitate easy removal of skin. Stone the fruit and chop into a liquidiser, blend to a purée. Choose ripe fruit for this. (Use small amounts only of plums as they might be laxative.)

Six to eight months:

As above plus these new suggestions:
Fresh fruit:
apples
banana
citrus

Finely grate a sweet eating apple and offer a little. Mash a ripe banana and add a little boiled (cold) water if too sticky to swallow. Seedless segments of orange, grapefruit, satsuma etc. can be offered.

Stewed fruit:
gooseberries
black/redcurrants

Stew the fruit and press through a nylon sieve to remove the seeds.

Raw purées:
melon
pineapple
cherries
oranges

Skin the fruits (except cherries) and remove any stones, pips, the central core in a pineapple and chop into a liquidiser; blend to a purée.

Yogurt:

Natural yogurt is best. If you do not make it at home (see recipe page 120) then choose a brand without any additives.

Fruit yogurt:	Home-made can be much nicer; just very finely chop a little fresh fruit into natural yogurt. Avoid shop-bought fruit yogurts with colouring, flavouring, stabilisers, preservatives etc., which means most commercial varieties. Make just before serving.
Yogurt purées:	Any of the fruit purées previously mentioned for this, or earlier age groups, can be mixed with a little natural yogurt.
Cottage, low-fat curd, fromage blanc, quark	All these low-fat cheeses can be mixed with fruit purées to make desserts or main courses for a baby. If using cottage cheese press it through a nylon sieve. Add fruit just before serving.

Eight months to family meals at between 15–18 months

As above plus these new suggestions:

Stewed fruit: blackberries raspberries loganberries tayberries	These fruits are suitable for stewing or using as raw purées. They should still be sieved until the baby is about 18 months when pips should be tolerated.
Raw purées: raspberries strawberries	Strawberries may cause an allergic rash in some babies so try only small amounts. Sieve raspberry purées until the baby is about 18 months.
Fresh fruit: most varieties grapes cherries	Fruit can now be introduced as finger food in small chunks or slices, without pips or seeds etc. Do not remove skins for finger foods, but wash very well. Seedless grapes or halved, deseeded grapes, can be offered, as can stoned cherries.
Yogurt:	Slightly more sophisticated yogurt-based mousses, whips and purées can now be offered if the family are having them as desserts..
Custards:	Home-made egg custards can now be introduced if baby is tolerating whole eggs. These can be made with milk or in the Indian style with yogurt (see page 122).
Baked fruit: apple peaches apricots	Baked apples can be mashed for baby, as can a little baked peach (see page 45) if the family is having that as a dessert.

When introducing fruit as finger food in particular it is best to obtain organically-grown produce if at all possible. Organically grown is preferable because it does not use chemical sprays and fertilisers and especially because the skins will not have been sprayed with chemical substances that remain as residues.

Is there such a thing as a balanced diet?

It's all very well paying attention to the desserts you eat, but they should only be a small part of your diet. Sensible eating for the rest of the day is essential for health. Good health means feeling good and freeing yourself to be able to concentrate on your work, family, and friends without worrying about your health. Being at your best means you can give of your best. If heredity has given you a lower health potential then fueling your body with the right food should make it easier for your system, and you, to reach your full potential.

This is not to say that you should become faddist or over-concerned with food. Food is there to be enjoyed, not agonised over, but it does mean that if you take care that the sum total of your diet is good then you can indulge in whatever dietary indiscretions you are prone to (in moderation) without doing yourself any harm!

Here are five easy-to-remember points that you might find helpful when choosing the foods you eat. Aim for foods that are: 1. low in fat; 2. low in sugar; 3. low in salt; 4. high in fibre (while also low in fat and sugar); 5. unprocessed, and that means daily fresh fruit and vegetables which are high in fibre, vitamins and minerals. It also means getting into the habit of reading food labels to see where the hidden salt, fat and sugar are lurking and to take action to avoid them.

Remember that food doesn't work in isolation. If you do smoke try to give up – it's harming you and those around you who have to live in your smoke. Also take adequate exercise – just 15 minutes aerobic exercise a day is enough!

The Recipes

In most of the recipes in this book I have used powdered gelatine but just as good results can be obtained with the vegetable setting agents agar-agar and Gelozone. For method of use and amounts see below.

Setting Agent	Amount to Set 1 Pint	Method of Use
Agar-agar	*2 level teaspoons	Sprinkle onto cold water or other liquid before bringing to the boil, stirring all the time, to dissolve.
Gelozone	2 level teaspoons	Follow the directions on the packet: Mix to a smooth paste with a little cold water. Add to the rest of the liquid. Bring to the boil and simmer for two minutes.
Gelatine	3 level teaspoons	Follow the directions on the packet. Place the hot liquid in a container, sprinkle on the gelatine and stir briskly until the liquid is thoroughly mixed. You can also sprinkle onto cold liquid and leave to soak before bringing to the boil, stirring all the time, to dissolve.

It is probably best to dissolve the setting agents in a basin standing in a saucepan of boiling water rather than putting directly in a saucepan over heat. This is because such small amounts as a few tablespoons of liquid, in which recipes often require the setting agent to be dissolved, may catch easily on the base of the saucepan and burn.

*2 level teaspoons are often recommended, but I prefer a softer set where the setting agent is indiscernable: there is nothing worse than a rubbery mousse or soufflé. I have found in my recipes that $\frac{1}{2}$ teaspoon is often sufficient.

Fruit-based Desserts

Raspberry and Kiwi Dessert

ILLUSTRATED ON PAGE 31
80 calories per portion

The rich raspberry colour contrasts superbly with the green of the sliced kiwi fruits which, incidentally, I always want to call by the name under which I first met them – Chinese gooseberries. That sounds so much nicer than Kiwi fruit.

*350 g/12 oz frozen raspberries, thawed · 2 (100-g/4-oz) eating apples
juice of ½ lemon · 4 tablespoons cold water
150 ml/¼ pint redcurrant or red grape juice
15 g/½ oz powdered gelatine · 2 Kiwi fruit (Chinese gooseberries)*

*Redcurrant and Raspberry
Delight (page 36), Raspberry
and Kiwi Dessert (page 30),
Raspberries with Almond Jelly
(page 32)*

Purée the thawed raspberries in a liquidiser together with any juice made while thawing. Peel and slice the apples and sprinkle the lemon juice on them to prevent discoloration. Cook in the cold water in a saucepan until soft. Add to the raspberries and liquidise to a purée. Boil the redcurrant or red grape juice and place in a small basin. Sprinkle over the gelatine, stirring until dissolved. If the gelatine does not dissolve immediately stand the basin in a saucepan of boiling water and continue stirring until it does. Allow to cool. When on the point of setting stir into the puréed mixture. Pour into a large glass serving dish or individual dessert glasses (so you can appreciate the lovely colours) and place in the refrigerator to set. Before serving top with freshly cut slices of the Kiwi fruit. For those who have not used them before they do need peeling before use: the black pips inside are edible. **Serves 4**

Raspberries with Almond Jelly

I LLUSTRATED ON PAGE 31
80 calories per serving

This is an unusual and attractive dish that was inspired by Michel Guérard in his innovative *Cuisine Minceur*. The almond jelly complements the raspberries in flavour, colour and texture. Using skimmed milk powder makes a low-calorie dessert. I think it is the combination of the two that make it successful – the jelly might seem bland on its own.

300 ml/½ pint water
25 g/1 oz skimmed milk powder
½ teaspoon agar-agar or 2 teaspoons powdered gelatine
15 g/½ oz flaked almonds
2 drops natural bitter almond essence
2 teaspoons fructose
450 g/1 lb fresh raspberries

Measure the water into a jug and then pour 3 tablespoons from it into a small bowl. Stir the skimmed milk powder into the larger amount of water and sprinkle the agar-agar or gelatine onto the smaller amount, stirring well. Heat the reconstituted milk in a saucepan until it begins to boil then pour a little onto the soaked setting agent, stirring to dissolve. Pour the setting agent into the saucepan and mix in thoroughly. Add the flaked almonds, almond essence and fructose and stir well. Pour into a shallow dish (of about 23-cm/9-in diameter) and leave to set. Chill thoroughly.

To serve use a pastry or biscuit cutter and cut out shapes of jelly – half moons are especially effective – and arrange on four serving plates with the raspberries in the middle. **Serves 4**

Figs and Raspberry Sauce

ILLUSTRATED ON PAGES 34–5

90 calories per serving or 100 calories with the cheese or yogurt decoration

A smooth raspberry sauce goes well with figs because it is a good contrast of texture, colour and flavour.

12 fresh figs
1 quantity of Raspberry Sauce (page 113)
50 g/2 oz medium-fat curd cheese or
100 g/4 oz strained Greek yogurt (optional)

Place the figs in a bowl of boiling water for 2–3 minutes then plunge them into cold water and skin. Cut a cross in the top of each fig, slicing down almost to the base of the fruit. Using your thumbs and forefingers press into each quarter at the base to open the fruit like a flower. Make up the sauce according to the instructions and pour onto four serving plates and leave to cool.

The curd cheese can be placed in a small piping bag with a star nozzle and piped into rosettes which will sit inside the opened figs. Alternatively a teaspoonful or so of thick, strained Greek yogurt can be swirled onto the top of the open fruit. To finish place the decorated figs on top of the sauce. **Serves 4**

Overleaf: Hazel Gantois (page 41), Carob Pears (page 36), Figs and Raspberry Sauce (page 33), Mango and Strawberries (page 37)

Redcurrant and Raspberry Delight

<small>ILLUSTRATED ON PAGE 31</small>
80 calories per portion

This is a simple and traditional Scandinavian dessert in which a fruit purée is thickened with potato flour to give a soft-set fruity 'jelly'. It is usually served with whipped double cream, but is just as nice on its own or with creamy, strained Greek yogurt. Redcurrant juice is not essential, but it's nice. Lindavia redcurrant juice is imported from Germany and is available from health food shops, delicatessens and some supermarkets.

175 g/6 oz redcurrants
175 g/6 oz raspberries
50 g/2 oz fructose
150 ml/¼ pint redcurrant juice
1 tablespoon potato flour mixed with 4 tablespoons cold water

Wash the fruit and string the redcurrants using a fork, reserving four sprigs to place over the edge of the serving glass as decoration. Place the fruits in a saucepan over a low heat and simmer for 10 minutes. Remove from the heat and sieve. Return to the saucepan and add the fructose and the redcurrant juice then bring to the boil. Remove from the heat again and stir in the potato flour, stirring all the time. Return to the heat to thicken. Allow to cool and pour into four serving glasses. Chill before serving. **Serves 4**

Carob Pears

<small>ILLUSTRATED ON PAGES 34–5</small>
240 calories per pear

1 (100-g/4-oz) carob bar
2 tablespoons decaffeinated black coffee
25 g/1 oz unsalted butter or soft vegetable margarine
2 free-range eggs, separated
6 pears
50 g/2 oz toasted hazelnuts, chopped
2 strips angelica

Melt the carob bar and coffee together in the top of a double boiler or in a basin standing in a saucepan of hot water. Remove from the heat and stir in the butter or margarine. When the mixture has cooled beat in the egg yolks. Whisk the egg whites until stiff and beat in 2 tablespoons to lighten the mixture. Fold in the rest of the egg whites.

Peel the pears, leaving the stalks in place. Core the pears from the base and fill with the chopped hazelnuts. Place them on a serving dish and slowly spoon over the carob mousse mixture which will flow down the sides and cover the base of the serving dish. To make pear leaves, soak the angelica in hot water for a few minutes to soften. Flatten with a palette knive and cut into triangular leaves with a sharp knife. Pierce the sides of the pears near the top and place the leaves in position.
Serves 6

Mango and Strawberries

ILLUSTRATED ON PAGES 34–5
50 calories per portion

In late summer and early autumn the second crop of strawberries coincides with some lovely ripe mangoes. The flavours are both distinctive, but they go well together; add some peaches and you have a really exotic fruit salad.

1 ripe mango
225 g/8 oz fresh strawberries
2 fresh peaches
5 tablespoons orange juice

Peel the mango using a potato peeler and dice the flesh. Scrape off any flesh from the flat stone and reserve. Wash and hull the strawberries and put 75 g/3 oz with the mango pulp. Pour boiling water over the peaches and leave to stand for 3 minutes then plunge into cold water and skin. Place half a peach with the mango pulp and strawberries and blend in a liquidiser to a purée (or push through a sieve). If the strawberries are large halve them or cut into thirds. Slice the remaining peaches. Toss the prepared fruit together. Add the orange juice to the purée, stir well and pour over the fruit salad. **Serves 4**

Moroccan Oranges with Dates

ILLUSTRATED ON PAGE 39
80 calories per serving, plus 15 calories for each date

Attending a reception in Morocco I was offered the largest and most delicious fresh dates I have tasted, together with tiny rosewater-flavoured pastries. This dessert combines both flavours with juicy Moroccan oranges.

3 large oranges (Moroccan!)
2 tablespoons clear honey
1 teaspoon rosewater
generous pinch of ground cinnamon
about 225 g/8 oz fresh dates

Peel the oranges, removing all the white pith. Slice into rounds, removing the pips as you go, and place an equal number on four dessert plates. Heat the honey and rosewater in a saucepan and spoon over the sliced fruit. Sprinkle with cinnamon to taste and offer, separately, a bowl of fresh dates. **Serves 4**

Israeli Fruit Salad

ILLUSTRATED ON PAGE 39
130 calories per serving

1 large orange (Jaffa, of course!)
1 grapefruit
2 tablespoons clear honey
1 teaspoon rosewater
8 fresh dates
2 tablespoons desiccated coconut

Moroccan Oranges with Dates (page 38), Mango Salad (page 40), Israeli Fruit Salad (page 38)

Peel the fruit well, cutting away all the white pith and cut out the segments. Place an equal number of segments on four serving dishes. Heat the honey and rosewater and pour over the fruit. Carefully stone the dates leaving them as whole as possible and place two on the side of each plate. Sprinkle the coconut over the fruit slices. **Serves 4**

Mango Salad

ILLUSTRATED ON PAGE 39
90 calories per serving

This is a very simple mixture, but delicious.

1 ripe mango · 2 juicy oranges
8 fresh dates (optional)
150 ml/¼ pint fresh orange juice

Peel the mango using a potato peeler. Holding the fruit in one hand and a small sharp knife in the other, cut slices from the flat stone similar in shape to those of canned peaches. Place in a serving dish. Peel the oranges and remove all the white pith. Cut into thin, circular slices, removing the pips as you do so. Place in a circle of overlapping slices on top of the mango. If using the dates wash them and slice them into thin slivers and scatter across the top of the fruit. Finally pour the orange juice over the fruit. **Serves 4**

Hot Fruit

ILLUSTRATED ON PAGES 42–4

As well as compôtes and stewed fruit, hot baked fruit, grilled fruit and barbecued fruit all make delicious desserts. In each case it is important that the fruit should not be allowed to dry out. A basting marinade can be made, using orange juice mixed with pineapple juice and a little clear honey, and this can be brushed on the grilled or barbecued fruit as it is cooking.

For special occasions a little liqueur (such as Grand Marnier or Cointreau) can be added to the marinade and the fruit can be steeped in it for an hour or longer in the refrigerator before it is used.

Soft fruits are not suitable for grilling and barbecuing but the fruits that are especially delicious are: bananas, orange slices, halved peaches, halved nectarines, halved apricots, fresh pineapple slices and juicy pears.

When barbecuing outside in the summer you can use kebab skewers for fruit, cutting it into chunks large enough not to disintegrate when the skewer is passed through them. These can be turned easily and basted using a pastry brush.

Blackcurrant Brulée

ILLUSTRATED ON PAGES 42–3
110 calories per portion

A brulée is usually made with a layer of double cream or soured cream over a sweetened fruit dish, but the creamy texture of strained Greek yogurt, and its ability to hold together and not separate into curds and whey when heat is applied (as ordinary yogurt does) makes it a delicious and excellent substitute.

350 g/12 oz blackcurrants · 4 tablespoons cold water
225 g/8 oz strained Greek yogurt · 4 teaspoons demerara sugar (optional)

Wash the blackcurrants and top and tail them. Place in a saucepan with the cold water and cover. Bring slowly to simmering point and cook for 10 minutes. Spoon the blackcurrants and juice into four small ramekins. Top with the yogurt and sprinkle a teaspoonful of sugar over each. Place under a high grill for a few minutes until the sugar melts. Serve at once. **Serves 4**

Hazel Gantois

ILLUSTRATED ON PAGES 34–5
180 calories per biscuit

50 g/2 oz hazelnuts · 75 g/3 oz wholemeal flour
40 g/1½ oz soft vegetable margarine
1½ teaspoons concentrated apple juice · 1 tablespoon cold water

Lightly roast the hazelnuts under the grill, turning a couple of times until they are golden brown. Place the flour in a mixing bowl and rub in the fat until the mixture resembles fine breadcrumbs. Grind the roasted hazelnuts in a liquidiser, food processor or coffee mill and stir into the flour. Mix together the apple juice and water and use to bind the mixture together into a soft and dryish dough. Knead lightly then roll out on a floured surface to 5 mm/¼ in deep. Cut into four biscuits using a 7-cm/3-in biscuit cutter or cut into rectangles with a knife and place on a greased baking tray. Bake in a moderate oven (180 c, 350 f, gas 4) for 15 minutes. Leave on the baking tray until crisp and then turn out onto a wire rack to cool. **Makes 4**

Overleaf: *Hot Fruit (page 40),*
Golden Harvest (page 44),
Blackcurrant Brulée (page 41),
Pear and Fig Compote
(page 44)

Pear and Fig Compote

ILLUSTRATED ON PAGES 42–3
90 calories per serving

I originally made this as a breakfast dish but the flavours were so good together and fresh figs are rather a luxury, so it has now become a popular dessert!

2 firm pears
300 ml/½ pint water
3 tablespoons concentrated apple juice
1 cinnamon stick
4 allspice berries
8 fresh green figs

Peel the pears, halve and core them. Place in a saucepan with the water, apple juice, cinnamon and allspice. Cover and simmer for 20 minutes. Allow to cool in the liquid. To prepare the figs pour boiling water over them and leave for 2 minutes, then plunge into cold water and skin, using a sharp knife to scrape away the skin. Cut the figs in half. Alternatively the figs can be left unpeeled, but in this case wash them well first. Add the prepared figs to the compote while it is still hot.
Serves 4

Golden Harvest

ILLUSTRATED ON PAGES 42–3
100 calories per serving

The unusual combination of peaches and yellow plums makes not only a very attractive dessert, but a most delicious one. It's so simple, but so outstandingly good. . .

450 g/1 lb yellow plums
2 peaches
150 ml/¼ pint orange juice
juice of ½ lemon
2 tablespoons Grand Marnier or another orange liqueur

Place the plums and peaches in a bowl and pour over boiling water. Stand for 2 minutes then drain and plunge into cold water. The skins should now come off easily and the fruit can be stoned. Place the halved plums and the sliced peaches in the serving dish. In a saucepan place the orange juice, lemon juice and Grand Marnier and bring to the boil. Pour the hot syrup over the fruit and leave until cool. Chill, if liked, but I prefer this salad at room temperature to appreciate the full flavour and aroma of the fruit. **Serves 4**

Baked Peaches

ILLUSTRATED ON PAGE 46

115 calories per serving

This makes a lovely warm dessert at the end of the summer when evenings are cooler and peaches are often cheaper!

4 large juicy peaches
50 g/2 oz wholemeal digestive biscuit crumbs
100 g/4 oz curd cheese
1 free-range egg yolk
½ teaspoon natural bitter almond essence
4 tablespoons Lindavia apricot nectar drink

Lightly butter a shallow ovenproof dish large enough to accommodate eight peach halves in a single layer.

Skin the peaches by placing in a bowl and covering with boiling water for 2 minutes. Drain and plunge into cold water. The skins should now slip easily from the peaches. Cut them in half and remove the stone and scoop out a little more flesh to make a slightly bigger hole. In a basin mix together most of the crumbs (reserving some for sprinkling on top of the peaches) and the curd cheese, egg yolk, essence and apricot nectar. Place teaspoonfuls of the paste into the peaches and sprinkle with the reserved crumbs. Bake in a moderate oven (180 c, 350 f, gas 4) for 20 minutes. **Serves 4**

Fruit Jelly

ILLUSTRATED ON PAGE 46

Rather than using the rubbery cubes which contain artificial flavourings and colouring why not make fruit jellies in the old fashioned way using real fruit and fruit juices which are set with gelatine, or the vegetarian equivalents agar-agar or Gelozone? They are almost as simple to make as packet jelly and involve the same process of dissolving the setting agents in liquid then allowing it to re-set.

Making jellies by the natural method involves boiling the fruit juice and then either sprinkling on the gelatine and stirring to dissolve or mixing the Gelozone or agar-agar with some cold water before adding to the hot juice and stirring to dissolve.

To make the jellies more appealing and nutritious real fruit can be added. For example, if you use red grape juice then add some black grapes to the jelly when it is on the point of setting, or pour the jelly liquid over some fruit in individual serving glasses or a mould.

Use any combination of your choice. Here are a few ideas:

- white grape juice with green seedless grapes
- orange juice with segments of orange, tangerine, satsuma, mandarin
- grapefruit juice with strawberries
- red grape juice over blackcurrants or raspberries
- redcurrant juice with raspberries or redcurrants

The combinations are virtually endless, but there are a couple of fruits – pineapple and kiwi fruit – which contain enzymes that inhibit gelling agents. However, canned fruit may be used because it has been heated in the canning process thereby destroying the enzymes.

The amount of setting agent you use is a question of personal choice. Do you like a rubbery jelly or a soft-set jelly? See the notes in the glossary for an explanation of the differences between gelatine, agar-agar and Gelozone, or take a look at the table at the beginning of the recipes section.

Baked Peaches (page 45), Fruit Jelly (page 47), Cheese Platter (page 48)

Cheese Platters

ILLUSTRATED ON PAGE 46

Cottage Cheese

Cottage cheese can form the basis of some delicious desserts, especially for those who do not want the calories of full-fat or hard cheeses and for those who like a dessert but prefer something that is not too sweet.

One attractive combination is a small mound of cottage cheese in the centre of a dessert dish surounded by skinned segments of pink grapefruit, placed alternately with stewed prunes.

Slices of kiwi fruit, arranged in a ring around a mound of cottage cheese are attractive, especially when combined with fresh strawberries.

Black grapes and banana slices (tossed in lemon juice to prevent discoloration) are another popular combination.

All of the above make the most of complementary flavours and attractive colour mixes, which are two important elements to consider when making up your own platters.

Goat's Cheese

Stronger flavoured soft goats' cheeses, available in round 'logs' in many cheese shops and delicatessens as well as supermarkets, are excellent for those who like their cheese to have a good flavour, but who do not want to eat blue cheeses.

Ripe, but firm and juicy pears are excellent with these cheeses and firm, juicy nectarines also go well with them. Sliced fresh peaches are also nice with goats' cheeses.

All varieties of melon (except watermelon) also go well with this type of cheese.

Mousses, Whips and Soufflés

Tangerine and Lemon Mousse

ILLUSTRATED ON PAGE 51

55 calories per serving

This is a deliciously light citrus mousse with a creamy lemon tangy layer on top. The top layer is heavier than the bottom, so do not turn out of the moulds onto serving dishes until just before serving.

225 g/8 oz natural yogurt · 100 g/4 oz low-fat curd cheese
juice and rind of 1 large lemon
25 g/1 oz powdered gelatine or 1 teaspoon agar-agar
150 ml/¼ pint orange juice · 450 g/1 lb tangerines
1 free-range egg white

Fill six dariole moulds with cold water. Cream together the yogurt, curd cheese, lemon juice and rind, working slowly to ensure there are no lumps. Sprinkle the setting agent onto the cold orange juice in a saucepan and place over the heat. Bring to the boil, stirring to dissolve. Allow to cool. When on point of setting fold one-third into the cheese and yogurt mixture. While the setting agent is cooling, peel the tangerines, removing the pith and pips and placing the segments in a liquidiser. Blend to a purée. Pour the cold water out of the moulds and stand in a tray. Place the cheese and yogurt mixture in the moulds and put in the refrigerator for 20 minutes to firm and set. Add the remaining setting agent to the puréed tangerines and blend. Whisk the egg white until stiff and fold into the tangerine purée. Spoon on top of the setting yogurt mixture and return the moulds to the refrigerator to set and chill before serving. **Makes 6**

Mango Mousse

ILLUSTRATED ON PAGE 51

95 calories per serving

This has such a delicate flavour, aroma and colour that you must make it just once, even if you think mangoes a little extravagant. It has the added virtue of being very low in calories.

1 large ripe mango
225 g/8 oz strained Greek yogurt
15 g/½ oz powdered gelatine or ½ teaspoon agar-agar
150 ml/¼ pint orange juice
2 free-range egg whites
carob curls to decorate (optional)

Peel the mango and chop the flesh then place it in a liquidiser (the cook can enjoy sucking the large flat stone and getting off all the flesh!). Add the yogurt and blend to a purée. Sprinkle the setting agent onto the orange juice in a small saucepan and bring to the boil to dissolve, stirring all the time. Allow to cool (this is quicker if you pour the juice into a cold bowl standing in cold water). When on point of setting stir into the yogurt mixture. Whisk the egg whites until stiff and mix 2 tablespoons into the mixture to lighten it then fold in the remaining egg white. Pour into a large glass dish (so you appreciate the colour and texture) or place in six individual serving glasses. Refrigerate for 2 hours at least to set and chill. Decorate with curls of carob if desired. **Serves 6**

Note: The tiny fibres in the mango appear like little hairs in the mousse, but this is perfectly all right to eat!

Variation: 3 peaches can be substituted for the mango in this recipe to make a delicious Peach Mousse.

Tangerine and Lemon Mousse (page 49), Mango Mousse (page 50), Orange and Blackberry Mousse (page 52)

Orange and Blackberry Mousse

ILLUSTRATED ON PAGE 51

112 calories per serving

The custard makes this dessert deliciously smooth and the two flavours of orange and blackberry, although unlikely, combine well for a delicious dessert.

225 g/8 oz blackberries
2 free-range eggs, separated
½–1 tablespoon fructose
300 ml/½ pint skimmed milk
rind and juice of 1 orange
15 g/½ oz powdered gelatine or ½ teaspoon agar-agar

Wash the blackberries and liquidise. Sieve into a bowl. Beat the egg yolks and fructose together in a blender. Place the milk in a saucepan with the orange rind and bring to blood heat. Remove from the heat and pour a little onto the egg yolk mixture. Whisk again and pour into the saucepan with the rest of the milk. Return to the hob and heat, stirring continuously, until the custard thickens; do not boil because this will make the custard curdle. When thickened, after about 7–10 minutes, remove from the heat and pour into a basin. Stand in a bowl of cold water and stir to hasten cooling. Sprinkle the setting agent onto the orange juice in a small basin, place in a saucepan of boiling water and stir well until dissolved. Then allow to cool. When the custard has cooled stir it into the blackberry purée. When the setting agent is on the point of setting stir it into the purée, mixing well. Whisk the egg whites until stiff and mix 2 tablespoons into the blackberry mixture to lighten it. Fold in the rest of the whisked whites and pour into a mould or individual ramekins. Place in the refrigerator to set and chill. **Serves 4**

Blackcurrant Foam

ILLUSTRATED ON PAGES 54–5

90 calories per serving

The cassis used in this recipe replaces sugar and acts as a sweetener. It is a syrup made in France from blackcurrants and is available from some off-licences, delicatessens or supermarkets. Made without colouring, sirop de cassis contains concentrated blackcurrant juice and natural fruit extracts and sugar. Tofu helps give the dessert a creamy texture without adding any fat.

225 g/8 oz blackcurrants
4 tablespoons cold water
2 tablespoons cassis
15 g/½ oz powdered gelatine
4 tablespoons boiling water
100 g/4 oz strained Greek yogurt
100 g/4 oz tofu, drained
2 free-range egg whites

Wash then top and tail the blackcurrants. Place in a saucepan with the cold water and cook over a moderate heat for 5 minutes. Take off the heat and liquidise, then sieve. Cool slightly and stir in the cassis. Allow to cool further while preparing the gelatine by sprinkling onto the boiling water and dissolving. If the gelatine does not dissolve place the basin in a saucepan of boiling water and stir until dissolved. Remove and allow to cool. Mix together the yogurt and tofu and stir into the cool purée. When the gelatine is on the point of setting stir into the purée. Whisk the egg whites until stiff and mix in 2 tablespoons to lighten the mixture then fold in the remainder. **Serves 4**

Overleaf: *Blackcurrant Foam (page 53), Chestnut Whirl (page 56), Apricot and Lemon Cream (page 56)*

Chestnut Whirl

ILLUSTRATED ON PAGES 54–5

170 calories per serving

This dessert can also be used as a delicious cream filling for gâteaux or choux pastry.

1 (42-g/1½-oz) plain carob bar
2 tablespoons skimmed milk
175 g/6 oz chestnut purée
225 g/8 oz strained Greek yogurt
2 free-range egg whites
a little grated carob or pinch of ground cinnamon to decorate

Place the carob bar and milk in a saucepan and place over a moderate heat, stir until dissolved but do not boil. Remove from the heat and place in a food processor or liquidiser. Add the chestnut purée and blend to a smooth cream. When the mixture is cool add the yogurt and blend again. Whisk the egg whites until stiff. Remove the purée from the blender and mix in two tablespoons of egg white to lighten the mixture. Fold in the remaining egg white and spoon into four individual serving dishes or ramekins. Place in the refrigerator to chill. Just before serving decorate with a little grated carob or a pinch of ground cinnamon. **Serves 4**

Apricot and Lemon Cream

ILLUSTRATED ON PAGES 54–5

130 calories per serving

This is very similar to a fruit fool. Fools traditionally mix fruit purées with whipped double cream or thick custards, but by using yogurt you can achieve the same effect for virtually no fat and far fewer calories. Dried fruits such as apricots, peaches and prunes can make year-round desserts but fresh fruit purées (when the fruit is in season) are just as delicious and combine well with the thick, creamy, strained Greek yogurt. This recipe does not make large servings but the portions are creamy and rich.

225 g/8 oz dried apricots
225 g/8 oz strained Greek yogurt
juice and rind of 1 lemon
25 g/1 oz flaked almonds, toasted, to decorate

Wash the apricots well and place in a saucepan with plenty of boiling water. Simmer for 40 minutes until soft. Remove from the heat and place in a liquidiser, reserving the liquid in which they were cooked. Add enough of this liquid to blend the apricots to a thick purée. When cold add the yogurt, lemon juice and rind and blend again. Spoon into six small ramekins and place in the refrigerator to chill. Just before serving sprinkle with freshly toasted almond flakes. **Serves 6**

Hot Vanilla Soufflé

ILLUSTRATED ON PAGE 59
90 calories per serving

Delicious on its own or with any of the fruit sauces, especially plum, blackberry or orange.

2 teaspoons desiccated coconut
150 ml/¼ pint skimmed milk
½ vanilla pod
25 g/1 oz fructose
1 free-range egg
15 g/½ oz wholemeal flour
2 drops natural vanilla essence
2 free-range egg whites

Lightly butter four ramekins or individual soufflé dishes and dust evenly with the coconut. Place the milk and vanilla pod in a saucepan and bring slowly to simmering point. Remove from the heat. Whisk together the fructose, egg and flour in a blender, pour on a little of the milk, then pour back into the saucepan, and stir until the mixture has thickened. Add the vanilla essence. Whisk the egg whites until stiff and fold into the custard. Pour into the dishes and bake in a moderately hot oven (190 c, 375 f, gas 5) for 25 minutes, until risen and golden brown. Serve at once. **Makes 4**

Blackcurrant Soufflé

ILLUSTRATED ON PAGE 59

190 calories per portion

This soufflé recipe uses fewer eggs than a conventional recipe and it also replaces the double cream with creamy strained yogurt for a much lower calorie version of a classic dessert. The fruit purée gives it a good texture and it makes very good use of the natural sweetness of fruit, so cutting down on sugar.

225 g/8 oz blackcurrants
4 tablespoons cold water
15 g/½ oz powdered gelatine
2 free-range egg yolks
50 g/2 oz fructose
225 g/8 oz strained Greek yogurt
3 free-range egg whites
about 100 g/4 oz curd cheese to decorate (optional)

Prepare a small soufflé dish by making a paper collar. To do this cut a strip of greaseproof paper of double thickness to go around the dish and overlap. It must also be raised 5 cm/2 in above the top of the dish. Fix in place with string or sticky tape.

Top and tail the blackcurrants then place in a saucepan with the water and bring to simmering point, simmer for 10 minutes. Remove from the saucepan and cool. Sprinkle the gelatine onto 4 tablespoons of the hot cooking liquid and stir to dissolve, place over hot water and stir if it does not dissolve readily, then cool. Liquidise, but do not sieve. Whisk together the egg yolks and the fructose until thick and creamy then whisk the purée into this mixture.

Fold the yogurt into the purée and when the gelatine is on the point of setting stir it into the mixture. Whisk the egg whites until stiff and mix in 2 tablespoons to lighten the mixture, then fold in the remainder. Place gently in the soufflé dish and chill until set. Before serving, carefully ease off the greasepoof paper collar and decorate with rosettes of curd cheese piped around the edge if desired. **Serves 4**

Blackcurrant Soufflé (page 58),
Hot Vanilla Soufflé (page 57)

Passion Fruit and Pomegranate Soufflé

105 calories per serving

This might seem an unusual combination of ingredients but the passion fruit and pomegranate are related botanically and so the hunch that their flavours might therefore go well together was well repaid in the tasting of this lighter-than-air fantasy.

4 passion fruit
1 pomegranate
2 free-range eggs, separated
2 tablespoons fructose

Lightly butter four small ramekins and stand them in a roasting tin.

Halve the fruits and spoon the pulp into a sieve, work out all the juice using a wooden spoon; don't forget to also collect the pulp from beneath the sieve. Whisk together the egg yolks and the sugar until thick and creamy then mix in the fruit juice. Whisk the egg whites until stiff and then fold into the fruit juice mixture. Spoon into the prepared ramekins and pour boiling water into the tin to come halfway up the sides of the ramekins. Cook for 20 minutes in a moderate oven (180 c, 350 f, gas 4) until risen and a dark golden brown on top. Serve at once. **Serves 4**

Note: The mixture does look a dull greyish colour initially but it bakes to a more frivolous fawn.

Iced Desserts

Melon Sorbet

ILLUSTRATED ON PAGE 63
35 calories per scoop

1 large galia (or other scented) melon
150 ml/¼ pint cold water
1 tablespoon fructose
2 free-range egg whites, whisked

Quarter the melon and remove the seeds. Roughly chop the flesh and place in a liquidiser with the water and fructose and blend to a purée. Pour into a shallow tray and place in the freezer. When almost frozen, remove and break up with a fork, mashing well. Fold in the whisked egg whites and return to the freezer in a container deep enough to allow scoops to be taken for serving. Remove from the freezer 20 minutes before serving to soften enough for the scoops to be taken. **Makes 8 scoops**

Mango Sorbet

ILLUSTRATED ON PAGE 63

65 calories per scoop

2 ripe mangoes
juice of 1 orange
2 tablespoons fructose
150 ml/¼ pint hot water
2 free-range egg whites

Peel the mangoes and cut the flesh into chunks and place in a liquidiser. Add the juice of the orange and blend to a purée. Dissolve the fructose in the water and pour into the mango purée. Pour into a shallow tray and place in the freezer until the mixture is just frozen then remove and break up with a fork, mashing well. Fold in the whisked egg white and pour into a container that is deep enough to allow scoops to be taken from it when the sorbet has frozen. Remove from the freezer for about 20–30 minutes before serving to allow the sorbet to soften slightly. **Makes 8 scoops**

Variation: For a lime sorbet add the juice from 3 limes plus the grated rind of 1 lime to the fructose dissolved in the hot water. Omit the orange juice and follow the method above.

Pineapple Foam Sorbet

ILLUSTRATED ON PAGE 63

35 calories per scoop

1 ripe pineapple
1 tablespoon clear honey
2 free-range egg whites, whisked

Mango Sorbet (page 62), Melon Sorbet (page 61), Raspberry Smetana Sorbet (page 64), Pineapple Foam Sorbet (page 62)

Peel the pineapple and chop the flesh roughly into a liquidiser. Blend to a smooth, foamy purée and pass through a sieve into a bowl. Stir in the honey and pour into a shallow container and place in the freezer. When nearly frozen remove and break up with a fork, mashing well, then fold in the whisked egg whites and return to the freezer in a container that is deep enough to allow scoops to be taken for serving. Remove from the freezer 20 minutes before serving to soften slightly. **Makes 8 scoops**

Raspberry Smetana Sorbet

ILLUSTRATED ON PAGE 63

50 calories per serving

This is very quick to make and so simple that it's real child's play. It makes use of creamy, low-calorie smetana which is a cultured milk product similar to yogurt and available in health food shops, some supermarkets and Israeli or Eastern European food stockists, but cultured buttermilk could be used in place of smetana. The sorbet will set quicker if frozen raspberries that are only slightly thawed are used.

225 g/8 oz frozen raspberries, slightly thawed
300 ml/½ pint smetana or cultured buttermilk
2 free-range egg whites

Liquidise the raspberries and smetana and pour into a shallow ice tray. Freeze until lightly set: about 1 hour. Remove from the freezer, break up and liquidise. Whisk the egg whites until stiff and mix in 2 tablespoons to lighten the mixture, then fold in the remainder. Pour into a container and return to the freezer. Remove from the freezer about 20 minutes before serving to allow the sorbet to soften slightly. **Serves 4**

Blackberry Buttermilk Ice

ILLUSTRATED ON PAGE 67

80 calories per serving

Cultured buttermilk is another good substitute for double cream in ice-cream. Although it does not have the same texture as cream it does have a good flavour. Use one of the thicker varieties, like Raines. If buttermilk is unobtainable substitute with natural yogurt or creamed smetana which is also a cultured milk product deriving from Bulgaria. It has a thicker texture than yogurt and does not separate out into curds and whey so easily as yogurt. It is also creamier.

450 g/1 lb blackberries
225 g/8 oz cooking apples
300 ml/½ pint buttermilk, smetana or yogurt
2 free-range egg whites

Wash and pick over the blackberries. Place in a saucepan with the washed, cored and chopped apple, plus a few tablespoons of cold water. Bring to simmering point and cook for 10 minutes. Cool then liquidise. When cold stir in the buttermilk and pour into a shallow tray and freeze for 1 hour until lightly set. Whisk the egg whites until stiff. Place the blackberry freeze in the liquidiser and blend to a frozen mush. Pour into a bowl and mix in 2 tablespoons of the egg white to lighten the mixture. Fold in the remaining whisked white and pour into a container to freeze. Remove from the freezer 20 minutes or so before use, so it is soft enough to scoop out and serve. **Serves 4**

Ginger and Honey Ice Cream

63 calories per scoop

300 ml/½ pint skimmed milk
½ vanilla pod
1 free-range egg
1 free-range egg yolk
2 tablespoons clear honey
300 ml/½ pint strained Greek yogurt
2 pieces preserved stem ginger in honey

Place the milk in a saucepan with the vanilla pod cut in half lengthways so that it releases more of its flavour. Place over the heat and gradually bring to the boil. As soon as the milk boils remove from the heat, cover and leave to infuse for 15 minutes. Whisk together the egg, egg yolk and honey. Remove the vanilla pod from the milk and whisk it into the egg mixture. Return to a clean saucepan (if the milk pan is re-used the milk on the bottom might catch and burn giving the custard an unpleasant flavour), strain through a sieve and stir over a moderate heat until the custard thickens enough to coat the back of a spoon. Do not boil or the mixture will curdle. Remove from the heat and allow to cool. When cold fold in the yogurt. Grate the stem ginger very finely and fold into the mixture together with a tablespoon of the honey from the jar, if liked. Pour into a container and freeze. When nearly frozen remove from the freezer, break up with a fork and mash well. Return and re-freeze. **Makes 10 scoops**

Blackberry Buttermilk Ice (page 65), Brown Bread Ice Cream (page 68), Prune and Armagnac Ice Cream (page 68)

Prune and Armagnac Ice Cream

ILLUSTRATED ON PAGE 67

105 calories per scoop

I once tasted this delicious combination at a hotel in Brittany where the ice-cream was served with hot, freshly baked galettes, a specialist Breton biscuit. When I arrived home from holiday I started trying to reproduce the flavour of that ice-cream, and this is pretty near it!

225 g/8 oz prunes
300 ml/½ pint strained Greek yogurt
3 tablespoons Armagnac
2 free-range egg whites
150 ml/¼ pint soured cream

Cook the prunes in water until soft and, when cool enough to handle, remove the stones. Place the stoned prunes in a liquidiser with the yogurt and Armagnac and blend to a purée. Whisk the egg whites until stiff. Mix the soured cream into the prune mixture then fold in the whisked egg whites, pour into a container and freeze. Just before it is completely frozen remove and break up with a fork, mash well and return to the freezer in a container that is deep enough to allow scoops to be taken. Remove the ice-cream from the freezer 20 minutes before serving to allow it to soften sufficiently for scoops to be taken. **Makes 10 scoops**

Brown Bread Ice Cream

ILLUSTRATED ON PAGE 67

115 calories per scoop

75 g/3 oz wholemeal breadcrumbs
50 g/2 oz demerara sugar
300 ml/½ pint strained Greek yogurt
3 drops natural vanilla essence
2 free-range egg whites

Mix together the breadcrumbs and sugar and place in a grill pan. Toast well, stirring from time to time. Remove and cool. Place the yogurt in a basin and stir in the vanilla essence and the cooled breadcrumb mixture. Whisk the whites until stiff and fold into the mixture. Pour into a shallow tray and freeze. When on the point of freezing remove and break up well with a fork. Return to the freezer in a container that is deep enough to allow scoops to be taken. Remove the ice-cream from the freezer about 20 minutes before serving to allow it to soften sufficiently for scoops to be taken. **Makes 6 scoops**

Pistachio Ice Cream

ILLUSTRATED ON PAGE 70

135 calories per scoop

100 g/4 oz unsalted and unshelled pistachio nuts
300 ml/½ pint skimmed milk
½ vanilla pod
2 free-range eggs, 1 separated
2 tablespoons clear honey
225 g/8 oz strained Greek yogurt

Shell the nuts and roughly chop half, then grind the other half to a fine powder. Place the milk in a saucepan with the vanilla pod, which can be cut in half lengthways so it releases more of its flavour. Place over the heat and gradually bring to the boil. As soon as the milk boils remove from the heat. Cover and leave to infuse for 15 minutes, then remove the vanilla pod. Whisk together 1 egg, the egg yolk and honey and whisk in the milk. Sieve and return to a clean saucepan and stir over a moderate heat until the custard thickens enough to coat the back of a spoon. Do not boil or the mixture will curdle. Remove from the heat and allow to cool. Meanwhile whisk the reserved egg white. When cold fold in the yogurt, the whisked egg white and nuts then place in a container and freeze. **Makes 8 scoops**

Hazelnut Ice Cream

ILLUSTRATED ON PAGE 70

100 calories per scoop

300 ml/½ pint skimmed milk · ½ vanilla pod
1 free-range egg · 1 free-range egg yolk
2 tablespoons clear honey
50 g/2 oz toasted hazelnuts, chopped
50 g/2 oz ground hazelnuts
300 ml/½ pint strained Greek yogurt

Place the milk in a saucepan with the vanilla pod, which can be cut in half lengthways to release more of its flavour. Place over the heat and gradually bring to the boil. As soon as the milk boils remove from the heat, cover and leave to infuse for 15 minutes. Whisk together the egg, egg yolk and honey. Remove the vanilla pod from the milk, then whisk the milk into the egg mixture. Sieve and return to a clean saucepan then stir over a moderate heat until the custard thickens enough to coat the back of a spoon. Do not boil or the mixture will curdle. Remove from the heat and allow to cool. Fold in the nuts and yogurt and pour into a shallow tray and freeze. When the mixture is nearly frozen remove from the freezer and break up with a fork, mashing well. Return to a container that is deep enough to allow scoops to be taken from the frozen mixture. Remove from the freezer about 20 minutes before serving to allow the ice-cream to soften enough for scoops to be taken.
Makes 8 scoops

Bombes

Ice-cream bombes are great fun and always popular at parties and special occasions. Usually three layers are used, and one good flavour combination is the ginger and honey ice-cream with a pistachio layer and a mango layer. Or what about prune and Armagnac ice cream with a layer each of hazelnut and mango? Both these suggestions also give contrasting colours which is important when making a bombe.

The ice-cream is made and when it is firm, but not frozen, a layer of ice-cream is packed around the edge of the bombe (mould). The bombe is then placed in the freezer until the first layer is solid and then the second layer of ice-cream can be added, leaving a hollow in the middle which is filled with the third type.

Hazelnut Ice Cream (page 71),
Ice Cream Bombe (page 71),
Pistachio Ice Cream (page 69)

Cheesecakes and Fruit Terrines

Peach and Carob Cheesecake

ILLUSTRATED ON PAGE 75

150 calories per serving

175 g/6 oz wholemeal digestive biscuits
1 (42-g/1½-oz) plain carob bar · 4 tablespoons skimmed milk
3 peaches · 225 g/8 oz low-fat curd cheese
4 tablespoons orange juice
15 g/½ oz powdered gelatine
peach slices to decorate (optional)

Lightly grease a 20-cm/8-in springform or loose-bottomed cake or flan tin. Crush the biscuits to crumbs by placing in a polythene bag and pounding with a rolling pin, Place the carob bar and the milk in a saucepan and melt over a low heat, stir well and pour into a mixing bowl with the biscuit crumbs. Mix well then press the mixture into the base of the tin. Cool then chill in the refrigerator. Skin the peaches. If they are not ripe enough for the skins to come off easily pour over boiling water and leave them to stand for 2 minutes before plunging into cold water. The skins should then come off easily. Roughly chop and place in a liquidiser or food processor and blend to a purée. Put the cheese in a mixing bowl and stir in the purée. Place the orange juice in a saucepan and sprinkle on the gelatine. Place over a moderate heat and stir until dissolved. Allow to cool and when on the point of setting stir thoroughly into the cheese mixture. Grate in the half a carob bar and stir well. Pour onto the prepared base and return to the refrigerator to set and chill. Decorate the cheesecake with slices of peach arranged around the edge, if liked, before serving. **Serves 6**

Blushing Cheesecake

ILLUSTRATED ON PAGE 75

150 calories per serving

This cheesecake gets its name from the fact that the layer of strawberries placed near the top of the mixture 'blush' through the guava as the cheesecake cooks. It is absolutely delicious.

225 g/8 oz wholemeal digestive biscuits
40 g/1½ oz soft vegetable margarine
4 guavas
225 g/8 oz medium-fat curd cheese
225 g/8 oz quark or similar low-fat soft white cheese
2 free-range eggs, separated
juice of ½ lemon
100 g/4 oz strawberries

Lightly grease a 20-cm/8-in loose-bottomed cake or flan tin. Crush the biscuits to crumbs by placing them in a polythene bag and pounding with a rolling pin. Melt the margarine in a saucepan then pour onto the biscuits and press the mixture into the base of the prepared tin.

Peel the guavas and quarter the fruit – do not bother to remove the pips. (Isn't the aroma divine!) Place in a little water in a saucepan and poach for 15 minutes. Drain, reserving the liquid for a fruit salad dressing. Cool slightly and liquidise the fruit to a pulp. Sieve and place in a mixing bowl with the cheeses, egg yolks and lemon juice then mix thoroughly. Whisk the egg whites until stiff then mix in 2 tablespoons to lighten the mixture. Fold in the remainder. Pour most of the mixture on top of the prepared base, reserving a little. Wash and dry the strawberries. Hull them and slice lengthways. Place a layer of sliced strawberries on top of the mixture and top with the remaining cheesecake mixture. Bake in the centre of a moderate oven (180 c, 350 f, gas 4) for 40–45 minutes or until set and just starting to brown. Remove from the oven and cool on a wire rack. Chill slightly before serving, if liked. I prefer this at room temperature. **Serves 12**

Traditional Currant Cheesecake

ILLUSTRATED ON PAGE 75

160 calories per portion

BASE

225 g/8 oz digestive wholemeal biscuits
50 g/2 oz soft vegetable margarine
pinch of ground cinnamon

FILLING

450 g/1 lb cottage cheese
300 ml/½ pint natural yogurt
300 ml/½ pint soured cream
100 g/4 oz currants
15 g/½ oz powdered gelatine
4 tablespoons boiling water

Lightly grease a 23-cm/8-in loose-bottomed cake or flan ring. Crush the biscuits into crumbs. Melt the margarine in a saucepan over a low heat. Stir the cinnamon into the biscuits. Mix in the margarine and press the mixture into the base of the flan ring and place in the refrigerator to chill well.

Sieve the cottage cheese into a mixing bowl and stir in the yogurt and soured cream until smooth and well mixed. Add the currants. In a small basin sprinkle the gelatine onto the boiling water and stir until dissolved. If the gelatine does not dissolve stand the basin in a saucepan of boiling water. Allow to cool then, when on the point of setting, stir into the cheesecake mixture and pour onto the prepared base. Leave in the refrigerator to set. **Serves 10**

Traditional Currant Cheesecake
(page 74), Peach and Carob
Cheesecake (page 72), Blushing
Cheesecake (page 73)

Lime Cheesecake

ILLUSTRATED ON PAGES 78–9

200 calories per portion

I like this cheesecake because it is unusual in that it 'sits' on a flapjack-style base which is nice and crunchy. The lime also gives a refreshing flavour and, for a cheesecake, it is low in calories. I have made it in a heart-shaped flan ring because it makes an attractive change from the usual round or rectangular cheesecakes and it looks very pretty when decorated with thin slices of lime.

BASE

50 g/2 oz soft vegetable margarine
1 tablespoon clear honey
25 g/1 oz demerara sugar
175 g/6 oz porridge oats

FILLING

225 g/8 oz quark or similar low-fat soft white cheese
225 g/8 oz strained Greek yogurt
2 free-range eggs, separated
50 g/2 oz light muscovado sugar
grated rind and juice of 2 limes
15 g/$\frac{1}{2}$ oz powdered gelatine
4 tablespoons boiling water
thin slices of lime to decorate (optional)

Lightly grease a heart-shaped flan ring (or a 20-cm/8-in flan ring) and place on an oiled baking tray. Make sure the baking tray fits in your refrigerator because after cooking it will need to be cooled and placed in the refrigerator.

Melt the margarine, honey and sugar in a saucepan over a low heat. Stir in the oats. Press the mixture into the base of the flan ring and bake in the centre of a moderate oven (180c, 350f, gas 4) for 20 minutes. Remove and allow to cool, still on the baking tray, on a wire cooling rack.

Mix the cheese and yogurt together in a mixing bowl with the egg yolks and the sugar. Stir in the lime rind. Mix the lime juice with the boiling water in a small mixing bowl and sprinkle on the gelatine. Stand the bowl in a saucepan of boiling water and stir to dissolve the gelatine. Remove the bowl from the heat and leave to cool. When cool add to the cheese mixture, stirring well to ensure it is evenly mixed in. Whisk the egg whites until stiff then fold into the mixture with a metal spoon. When the cheese mixture is on the point of setting pour onto the prepared base and place in the refrigerator to set. **Serves 8**

Coeur à la Crème

ILLUSTRATED ON PAGES 78–9

60 calories per heart

This creamy cheese dish marries well with a tart fruit sauce, which I prefer rather than serving with whole fruit. Try any of the fruit sauces from the book with this recipe.

225 g/8 oz cottage cheese
225 g/8 oz quark or similar low-fat soft white cheese (or for a denser texture a low-fat curd cheese)
2 free-range egg whites

Line six *coeur à la crème* moulds with butter muslin and place on a baking tray with a raised edge that will fit in your refrigerator.

Sieve the cottage cheese into a mixing bowl and stir in the other cheese, mixing well. Whisk the whites until stiff, but not too dry and mix in 2 tablespoons into the mixture to lighten it. Fold in the remaining egg white and spoon into the prepared moulds. Chill in the refrigerator for at least 2 hours before serving. Unmould and peel off the muslin. Place directly on serving dishes or place on top of a layer of fruit sauce. **Serves 6**

Overleaf: *Strawberry Foam Pie (page 80), Lime Cheesecake (page 76), Coeur à la Crème with Blackberry and Apple, Victoria Plum and Raspberry Sauces (page 77)*

Strawberry Foam Pie

ILLUSTRATED ON PAGES 78–9
145 calories per serving

This is a really delicious and fruity dessert and it makes a most attractive dish when cut: with the dark hazelnut base topped with a layer of gooseberry cream and a layer of delicious strawberry foam.

50 g/2 oz hazelnuts
50 g/2 oz soft vegetable margarine
75 g/3 oz wholemeal flour
a little cold water to mix
350 g/12 oz gooseberries
2 teaspoons fructose
4 tablespoons cold water
15 g/½ oz powdered gelatine
4 tablespoons boiling water
225 g/8 oz strawberries
100 g/4 oz low-fat curd cheese
2 free-range egg whites

Lightly grease an 18-cm/7-in springform or loose-bottomed cake or flan tin. Toast the hazelnuts under the grill or in the oven. Remember to turn if toasting them. Allow to cool a little and grind in a coffee mill or liquidiser. Rub the margarine into the flour until the mixture resembles fine breadcrumbs. Stir in the ground hazelnuts and add enough cold water to make a soft dough. Roll out on a floured surface and then gently lift onto the prepared base using a palette knife because this is a very crumbly dough. Place the side of the springform tin in place. Prick the base all over with a fork and bake in a moderately hot oven (200 c, 400 f, gas 6) for 20 minutes. Remove and cool on a wire rack.

Simmer the gooseberries and fructose in the cold water in a saucepan over a moderate heat for 10 minutes. Allow to cool a little then liquidise. Sprinkle the gelatine onto the boiling water in a small basin and stand the basin in a saucepan of hot water. Stir until dissolved. Allow to cool. Wash and hull the strawberries and purée in a liquidiser. Pour into a dish. Place the cheese in a mixing bowl and gradually stir in the gooseberry purée ensuring the mixture remains smooth. When the

gelatine has cooled, pour half onto the gooseberry mixture and mix well. Pour on top of the biscuit base and place in the refrigerator to set for 10 minutes. Add the remaining gelatine to the strawberry mixture and mix in well. Whisk the egg whites until stiff and, using a metal tablespoon, mix 2 tablespoons into the strawberry purée to lighten the mixture. Fold in the remaining egg white and gently spoon on top of the set gooseberry layer. Return to the refrigerator to set for several hours before serving. **Serves 8**

Passion Fruit Curd Cake

ILLUSTRATED ON PAGE 83
140 calories per portion

In creating this cheesecake I wanted to get away from the biscuit or sponge base 'syndrome' and make a cheesecake more reminiscent of Yorkshire curd tarts, but with the exciting flavour of passion fruit.

2 tablespoons clear honey
2 free-range eggs
225 g/8 oz ricotta cheese
3 passion fruit
50 g/2 oz ground almonds
25 g/1 oz wholemeal semolina

Lightly grease a 20-cm/7-in sandwich tin. Place the honey and eggs in a bowl and whisk until thick and creamy. Whisk in the cheese and the pulp of the passion fruit. To remove the pulp halve the fruit and scoop out the pippy centre, which is the pulp, with a teaspoon. Add the almonds and the semolina and mix together well. Pour into the prepared tin and bake in a moderately hot oven (190 c, 375 f, gas 5) for 25 minutes until firm and set. Remove from the oven and allow to cool before removing from the tin.

This cheesecake can be served with a bowl of natural yogurt, if desired. **Serves 8**

Guava and Paw Paw Fruit Terrine

ILLUSTRATED ON PAGE 83

60 calories per serving

If you like guavas you'll love this one. Like the Lime and Kiwi Fruit Terrine the flavours complement each other superbly and the soft luscious texture of the juicy fruit is lovely inside the mousse. This one is a naturally sweet dessert without the tang of its kiwi and lime counterpart, but equally sophisticated.

2 guavas
225 g/8 oz strained Greek yogurt
4 tablespoons orange juice
15 g/½ oz powdered gelatine
2 free-range egg whites
1 paw paw

Line a 450-g/1-lb loaf tin with greaseproof paper. Peel the guavas and roughly chop into a liquidiser or food processor with the yogurt. Blend to a purée and rub it through a sieve to remove the pips. Place the orange juice in a saucepan and sprinkle on the gelatine, stir over a moderate heat until the gelatine has dissolved. Remove from the heat and cool. When on point of setting stir into the guava purée. Whisk the egg whites until stiff and fold into the purée. While the gelatine is cooling, peel and halve the paw paw. Scoop out and discard the black pips and slice the flesh into long thin strips. Pour one-third of the mousse into the tin and cover with a layer of paw paw strips, pour over another third of the mousse and repeat with the paw paw strips. Top with the remaining mousse and place in the refrigerator to set and chill. **Serves 8**

Passion Fruit Curd Cake (page 81), Lime and Kiwi Terrine (page 84), Guava and Paw Paw Terrine (page 82)

Lime and Kiwi Fruit Terrine

ILLUSTRATED ON PAGE 83

75 calories per serving

This is definitely a dessert for those with sophisticated tastes who like a tangy flavour. Be careful when removing from the tin. Cut into slices in the kitchen and serve the terrine on pretty dessert dishes. It needs careful cutting, so have a pie or fish slice on hand to support the slices.

2 limes
15 g/½ oz powdered gelatine
225 g/8 oz strained Greek yogurt
225 g/8 oz quark
2 kiwi fruit
2 free-range egg whites

Line a 450-g/1-lb loaf tin with greaseproof paper. Grate the zest from the limes into a bowl and squeeze the juice into a saucepan. Sprinkle on the gelatine and stir over a low heat until dissolved. Remove from the heat and allow to cool. Mix the yogurt and quark together with the lime zest. Peel the kiwi fruit and cut in half lengthways. Whisk the egg whites until stiff. Fold the cooled gelatine into the cheese mixture and when on point of setting fold in the whisked egg white. Pour half the mixture into the prepared tin and place the four kiwi halves, cut sides down, on top. Pour over the remaining lime mousse and place in the refrigerator to set and chill.

To remove from the tin place a flat plate over the base of the tin and invert gently. Carefully peel off the paper as you cut slices for serving, laying each slice flat on a dessert dish. **Serves 8**

Crepes

Basic Wholemeal Crepes

30 calories each

100 g/4 oz wholemeal flour
pinch of sea salt (optional)
1 free-range egg
300 ml/½ pint skimmed milk
4 tablespoons cold water

Place the flour in a mixing bowl with the sea salt, if wanted. Lightly beat the egg and place in a well in the centre of the flour. Using a fork, gradually beat the flour into the egg, working from the well towards the edge of the bowl, and add the milk as necessary. Finally add the water and whisk well with the fork.

Place a heavy based omelette pan over a high heat and add a few drops of soy or corn oil. When the oil is hot (but not smoking) add about 2 tablespoons of the batter, tipping the pan from side to side to ensure a thin, even layer. Cook until the batter has set then turn the crepe with a palette knife or fish slice. Cook for a minute or so then turn out onto a warmed plate. **Makes 14**

Recommended fillings: any of those in this chapter, especially nice as Crepes Suzette

Note: 2 tablespoons of skimmed dried milk powder whisked into 300 ml/½ pint cold water can be substituted for the skimmed milk in this recipe. This produces a slightly lighter crepe.

Breton Crepes

ILLUSTRATED ON PAGE 86

40 calories per crepe

2 free-range eggs
1 tablespoon vegetable, soy or corn oil
4½ tablespoons dry cider
100 g/4 oz buckwheat flour
175 ml/6 fl oz water

Lightly beat the eggs and mix in the oil and cider. Sieve the flour into a mixing bowl and make a well in the centre. Add the egg mixture and, using a fork, gradually begin to beat the flour into the egg working slowly from the well towards the edge of the bowl, adding the extra water to thin the mixture as you go. Give a final whisk with the fork before making the crepes. Cook in the same way as Basic Wholemeal Crepes, page 85. **Makes 14**

Recommended filling: Apple Streudel

Carob Crepes

ILLUSTRATED ON PAGE 86

55 calories per crepe

These are a dark chocolate-coloured brown with a carob aroma. Use a slightly lower heat than for other crepes because they burn quite easily.

75 g/3 oz wholemeal flour · 25 g/1 oz carob powder
1 free-range egg · 300 ml/½ pint skimmed milk

Sieve together the flour and carob powder and place in a bowl. Lightly beat the egg and place in a well in the centre of the flour. Using a fork gradually begin to beat the flour into the egg, working slowly from the well towards the edge of the bowl, adding milk as necessary to thin the mixture. Give a final whisk when all the liquid is combined. Cook in the same way as Basic Wholemeal Crepes, page 85. **Makes 14**

Recommended fillings: Coffee and Chestnut, Coconut, Orange Foam Sauce

Carob Crepes with Coffee and Chestnut Filling (pages 87 & 89), Breton Crepes with Apple Streudel Filling (pages 87 & 88), Crepes Suzette (page 89)

Apple Streudel Filling

ILLUSTRATED ON PAGE 86

60 calories per serving

These are wonderful served hot on a cold winter's day.

350 g/12 oz cooking apples
juice of ½ lemon
50 g/2 oz sultanas
25 g/1 oz walnuts
½ teaspoon ground cinnamon
3 tablespoons cold water
50 g/2 oz wholemeal breadcrumbs

Peel the apple and core. Chop roughly and place in a stainless steel or glass saucepan with the lemon juice, toss to prevent browning. (Do not use an aluminium saucepan because fruit can cause minute amounts of aluminium to be eroded into the fruit and this may be dangerous to health.) Mix in the sultanas. Chop the walnuts finely and add to the apple with the cinnamon and water. Cover and simmer for 15 minutes; check from time to time that the apple is not cooking too fast and burning or sticking to the base of the saucepan; if necessary add a little water. Remove from the heat and stir in the breadcrumbs. Stuff warm crepes, rolling them around the filling. **Makes enough to generously stuff 8 crepes**

Coconut Yogurt Filling

50 calories per serving

225 g/8 oz strained Greek yogurt
2 drops natural vanilla essence
2 tablespoons desiccated coconut

Place the yogurt in a bowl and cream in the vanilla essence and desiccated coconut. Easy, isn't it! **Makes enough for 8 crepes**

Coffee and Chestnut Filling

ILLUSTRATED ON PAGE 86

50 calories for each serving of stuffing

1 tablespoon decaffeinated coffee granules
1 tablespoon boiling water
100 g/4 oz chestnut purée
100 g/4 oz strained Greek yogurt
1 tablespoon fructose

Dissolve the coffee granules in the water. Place the chestnut purée in a food processor or liquidiser and add the cooled coffee, yogurt and fructose. Blend to a smooth purée. This is delicious chilled and spread on hot crepes. **Makes enough for 8 crepes**

Crepes Suzette

ILLUSTRATED ON PAGE 86

About 60 calories per crepe, including sauce

1 quantity of Basic Wholemeal Crepes (page 85)
2 large juicy oranges
1 large lemon
1 tablespoon Cointreau or Grand Marnier

Squeeze the juice from the fruit and mix in with the Cointreau or Grand Marnier. Return the folded crepes to the pan and pour over the liquid. Heat through.

Choux Pastries

Choux Buns

ILLUSTRATED ON PAGE 90
160 calories per bun

These can be filled with any of the fillings in this chapter or with fillings from the chapter on custards and creams.

150 ml/¼ pint water · 50 g/2 oz unsalted butter
100 g/4 oz 85 per cent wholemeal flour
2 free-range eggs, lightly beaten

Lightly grease two or three baking trays. Place the water and butter in a saucepan and bring to the boil. Stir to melt the butter and then add the flour and beat vigorously with a wooden spoon until the mixture leaves the sides of the saucepan in a smooth, shiny ball. Leave for 3 minutes to cool before gradually beating in the eggs. Beat between additions until the paste is stiff and the egg well combined. Place the paste in a piping bag fitted with a 1-cm/½-in plain nozzle and pipe 16 balls onto the baking trays. Leave space between the balls because they will rise. Glaze with lightly beaten egg or milk and bake in a moderately hot oven (200 c, 400 f, gas 6) for 20 minutes. Test to see if the centre is cooked, then cool on a wire rack. If a natural split has not already occurred during baking, make a split near the base of the buns for the steam to escape during cooling and drying. **Makes 16**

Note: It is important to use 85 per cent wholemeal flour not 100 per cent as the latter does not allow the choux pastry to rise sufficiently.

Strawberry Paris Brest (page 93), Chestnut Choux Rings (page 92), Choux Buns with Confectioner's Custard and Peach and Raspberry Sauce (pages 91, 117 & 116)

Chestnut Choux Rings

ILLUSTRATED ON PAGE 90
100 calories per ring

This is a variation in the shape of choux pastry. The paste is piped into small rings which are filled with a chestnut cream and melted plain carob is piped over the top.

1 quantity of choux pastry (page 91)
1 beaten egg or a little milk to glaze
15 g/½ oz flaked almonds
100 g/4 oz chestnut purée · 175 g/6 oz natural yogurt
3 tablespoons boiling water
1½ teaspoons powdered gelatine or ½ teaspoon agar-agar
1 tablespoon maple syrup
½ (42-g/1½-oz) bar plain carob
2 tablespoons skimmed milk

Make the choux pastry as instructed on page 91 but, instead of piping into buns, pipe into 7.5-cm/3-in circles using a 5-mm/¼-in plain piping nozzle; the mixture should make about 15 rings. Glaze the rings with lightly beaten egg or milk and sprinkle over the almonds. Bake for 20 minutes until cooked and hollow. Cool on a wire cooling rack.

To make the filling place the chestnut purée and yogurt in a liquidiser and blend to a purée. Place 2 tablespoons of the boiling water in a bowl and spinkle on the gelatine, stirring to dissolve: add the remaining tablespoon of water to help dissolve the gelatine. Leave to cool. Add the maple syrup to the chestnut purée. When the gelatine is on the point of setting fold into the chestnut mixture and place in the refrigerator for about 20 minutes to set. Place the carob in a saucepan with the milk and melt over a gentle heat. Make a small icing bag by rolling a piece of greaseproof paper into a cone and drop into it a piping nozzle with the finest writing point. Fold over the top of the paper to secure the cone. Spoon the carob into the bag. Slice the cooled rings in half horizontally. Spoon the chestnut mixture onto the base of each ring and place the top half in position. Place the filled rings together on the wire tray and drizzle the carob over the rings in a zig-zag pattern.
Makes 15

Note: Only about a quarter of a carob bar is needed to decorate the top but you need to use half a bar to enable enough to be spooned into the piping bag to make it work.

Strawberry Paris-Brest

ILLUSTRATED ON PAGE 90

190 calories per portion

The Paris-Brest is a large choux pastry ring of about 20-cm/8-in. in diameter. The story is that in the late nineteenth century the dessert was created in honour of a very famous bicycle race which ran on a circular route from Paris to Brest and back. Instead of the usual sweetened Chantilly Cream used to fill the ring, which is then dredged with icing sugar, I have used a low-calorie yogurt, cheese and strawberry purée as a filling and topped the dessert with sliced strawberries.

1 quantity of choux pastry (page 91)
100 g/4 oz cottage cheese
100 g/4 oz strained Greek yogurt
225 g/8 oz strawberries, washed and hulled
1½ teaspoons powdered gelatine
3 tablespoons boiling water

Lightly grease a baking tray. Make the choux pastry in the usual way described on page 91. Place the pastry in a piping bag fitted with a 1-cm/½-in plain nozzle and pipe a round of about 20-cm/8-in. in diameter onto a lightly oiled or non-stick baking tray, glaze and bake in a moderately hot oven (200c, 400f, gas 6) for 20–25 minutes. When cooked and hollow inside, remove and cool on a wire cooling rack.

Place the cottage cheese, yogurt and half the strawberries in a liquidiser and blend to a smooth purée. Sprinkle the gelatine onto the boiling water and stir to dissolve. Leave to cool. Finely dice half the remaining strawberries and fold into the strawberry purée together with the gelatine when it is on the point of setting. Place in the refrigerator to chill and set for about 20 minutes. Halve the cooled Paris-Brest horizontally and just before serving spoon the strawberry cream onto the base and place the top in position. Finely slice the remaining strawberries and place around the top of the Paris-Brest as decoration.
Serves 6

Raisin Puffs

50 calories per puff

Choux puffs are different from choux balls. They are larger and lighter. They are made from the same basic choux recipe, but by placing an upturned baking tin or loaf tin over the choux balls on the baking tray the steam is trapped during baking and the pastry rises to twice the size of an ordinary choux bun or éclair.

1 quantity of choux pastry (page 91)
225 g/8 oz low-fat curd cheese
50 g/2 oz raisins
1½ tablespoons concentrated apple juice
75 g/3 oz tofu

Make the choux pastry as described on page 91 and pipe the choux balls onto the baking trays, leaving room around them to place an up-turned baking or loaf tin over them. Bake in the same way as for choux buns and cool on a wire cooling rack.

To make the filling combine all the ingredients in a mixing bowl and mix thoroughly. Slice the tops off the puffs and fill each, when cold, with a spoonful of mixture.

As with the other choux recipes, any of the custards, creams or other fillings of choice may be used. **Makes 16**

Savarins

Basic Savarin Dough

140 calories per serving

225 g/8 oz wholemeal flour · 150 ml/¼ pint skimmed milk
15 g/½ oz fresh yeast or 1½ teaspoons dried yeast
1 (25 mg) vitamin C (ascorbic acid) tablet, crushed
1½ free-range eggs, lightly beaten
75 g/3 oz unsalted butter · 75 g/3 oz currants
1 quantity of Fruity Savarin Syrup or Honey Savarin Syrup (page 101)

Lightly grease a 23-cm/9-in savarin mould (or 10 brioche or small savarin moulds). Place the flour into a mixing bowl. Place the milk in a saucepan and heat until it is lukewarm. Remove from the heat and cream in the yeast and vitamin C tablet. Alternatively dissolve the dried yeast in the lukewarm milk, leave for 10 minutes, or until frothy, then add the vitamin C tablet. Beat in the eggs then pour the mixture into a well made in the flour. Beat for 5 minutes in an electric mixer. Melt the butter, but do not make it really hot, and pour it into the dough with the currants. Beat until all is absorbed. Fill the mould(s) one-third full and cover with a clean tea-towel. Leave to rise until it fills about two-thirds of the mould (this takes about 20 minutes in a warm room). Bake in a hot oven (220 c, 425 F, gas 7) for 25 minutes. Remove from the mould and place on a wire cooling rack over a plate and spoon over the hot syrup. The plate will collect the remaining syrup which can be spooned over again. Putting the syrup on when the savarin is hot gives the best results. Allow to cool. **Serves 10**

Savarin aux Fruits

ILLUSTRATED ON PAGES 98–9

175 calories per serving (including the savarin, filling and syrup)

Make one quantity of Basic Savarin Dough and soak it in the usual way; I think the Fruity Savarin Syrup is nicest with this recipe. Then make up a filling from the following:

1 small melon
1 (200-g/7-oz) can unsweetened pineapple rings or chunks
1 eating apple
3 tablespoons orange juice

Halve the melon and remove the pips. Using a parisienne cutter (melon baller) from one half cut large balls and from the other half use the other end of the cutter to cut smaller melon balls. Place them in a mixing bowl. Drain the pineapple and if it is in rings cut it into small chunks. Add to the melon. Wash the apple well and cube, tossing at once into the orange juice to prevent browning. Mix with the other fruit and pile into the centre of the savarin. **Serves 10**

Note: Fresh pineapple would be nicer in the salad, but for this small amount unsweetened pineapple canned in its own juice is more economical.

Dutch Apple Savarin

ILLUSTRATED ON PAGES 98–9

200 calories per serving (including savarin, filling and syrup)

Make one quantity of Basic Savarin Dough, omitting the currants, and for this savarin soak it in the sweeter Honey Savarin Syrup which contrasts well with the apples and spices. Then make up the filling from the following:

100 g/4 oz dried apricots
1 (225-g/8-oz) cooking apple
50 g/2 oz raisins
a small piece of stick cinnamon
2 allspice berries

Soak the apricots in boiling water for 30 minutes then cover in fresh boiling water in a saucepan, boil for 40 minutes then drain. Wash the apple well then quarter and core. Cut into thick, chunky slices and place in a saucepan with the apricots, raisins, cinnamon stick and allspice. Add 150 ml/¼ pint water and cover. Cook over a moderate heat for 15 minutes until the apple is cooked, but not too soft. Remove the cinnamon stick and allspice berries. Drain, if necessary, and pile into the centre of the savain. I prefer this served at room temperature, so you could allow the apple mixture to cool before placing in the savarin and serving. **Serves 10**

Pineapple Savarin

ILLUSTRATED ON PAGES 98–9
170 calories per serving (including savarin and glaze)

This savarin can be glazed with hot, no-added sugar apricot jam when it is removed from the oven, and brushed again with the glaze just before serving to give it an appetising appearance.

1 quantity of Basic Savarin Dough (page 95)
1 fresh pineapple (with handsome top leaves)
4 tablespoons no-added sugar apricot jam · a little kirsch (optional)

Make one quantity of Basic Savarin Dough omitting the currants and bake in the usual way (see page 95). When cold cut into slices of about 1-cm/½-in thickness.

Prepare the pineapple by cutting into slices of equal thickness, reserving the top. If you have not prepared a fresh pineapple before it is easier to cut it in half, horizontally, and cut off the top leaves, which should be reserved. Now cut away the tough outer skin, without removing too much flesh, by cutting from the narrower end downwards towards the board. Cut away all the inverted 'spikes' either with the end of a sharp knife or with tweezers, then slice into rounds. Cut out the central core: some people prefer to do this with a scone or biscuit cutter, personally I think it is easier with a knife.

Toast the slices of savarin on both sides until lightly browned and lay in a large circle on a serving dish, placing alternate slices of pineapple and savarin. Heat the apricot jam in a small saucepan and use to glaze the savarin then, if liked, sprinkle with a little kirsch. Use the reserved pineapple leaves to decorate the savarin. **Serves 10**

Overleaf: Dutch Apple Savarin (page 96), Savarin aux Fruits (page 96), Christmas Savarin (page 100), Pineapple Savarin (page 97)

Christmas Savarin

ILLUSTRATED ON PAGES 98–9

180 calories per serving

I have called this a Christmas Savarin because it makes use of the spices which we associate with Christmas baking. It is also richer than the Basic Savarin Dough and so should be used for special occasions only.

350 g/12 oz wholemeal flour · 1 teaspoon mixed spice
200 ml/10 fl oz skimmed milk
25 g/1 oz fresh yeast or 15 g/1½ oz dried yeast
1 (25 mg) vitamin C (ascorbic acid) tablet, crushed
1 tablespoon molasses
50 g/2 oz currants · 50 g/2 oz raisins
50 g/2 oz sultanas · 25 g/1 oz cut mixed peel
a little clear honey to glaze

Lightly grease a savarin mould. Place the flour and spice in a mixing bowl. Warm the milk until it is blood temperature and remove from the heat. Cream in the yeast, vitamin C tablet and molassses. Alternatively dissolve the dried yeast in the lukewarm milk, leave until frothy, then add the vitamin C tablet and molasses. Stir the dried fruit and mixed peel into the flour and add the milk. Form in to a soft dough and knead for 5 minutes. Place the dough in the mould and cover. Leave until the dough has nearly doubled in size then bake in a hot oven (220 c, 425 f, gas 7) for 20–25 minutes. Remove from the oven and, when cool enough to handle, remove from the mould and, using a pastry brush, glaze with a little clear honey. **Serves 10**

Fruity Savarin Syrup

8 calories per serving

This will give you enough syrup for one batch of dough. Unlike the usual sugar syrups it is very low in calories at about 85 for the batch which works out at around eight calories per serving.

4 tablespoons cold water
juice and zest of ½ orange
juice of ½ lemon
½ vanilla pod
1 tablespoon clear honey

Place all the ingredients in a saucepan over a moderate heat and cover. Simmer for 10 minutes. Remove the vanilla pod and pour over the savarin.

Honey Savarin Syrup

30 calories per serving

This is a slightly sweeter syrup, but it still retains its fruity zest. Contains around 300 calories, or 30 per serving. Still a relatively low-calorie delicious syrup!

4 tablespoons clear honey
juice and zest of 1 orange
juice of 1 lemon

Place all the ingredients in a saucepan over a moderate heat and cover. Simmer for 5 minutes, then pour over the savarin.

Gâteaux

Hazelnut and Nectarine Gâteau

ILLUSTRATED ON PAGE 102

85 calories each

2 free-range eggs
50 g/2 oz clear honey
1 tablespoon boiling water
75 g/3 oz ground hazelnuts
50 g/2 oz wholemeal flour
1 nectarine

Lightly grease eight individual cake tins of 9-cm/3½-in. in diameter and 5-cm/2-in depth. Whisk together the eggs and honey until thick and ropey. Add the boiling water and fold in the ground hazelnuts and flour using a metal tablespoon. Pour into the tins and bake in a moderate oven (180 c, 350 f, gas 4) for 18 minutes, until golden brown and springy to the touch. Cool on a wire rack for a few minutes before unmoulding.

To decorate wash, then cut the nectarine into quarters and cut each quarter in half, horizontally. Cut off thin fan-shaped slices and place in a circle around the top of the eight little gâteaux. **Makes 8**

Fresh Fruit Gâteau (page 104),
Hazelnut and Nectarine Gâteau
(page 103)

Fresh Fruit Gâteau

Illustrated on page 102

184 calories per serving

This is a lighter-than-light sponge base which is topped with fresh fruit. You can use any fruit, but I find the combination of black grapes and banana successful and it also looks good. Alternatively the gâteau may be cut in half and the fruit placed in the middle; this may be preferred because the gâteau has an excellent colour and the top should be completely level. Take care when cutting the gâteau horizontally because it is very light and crumbly, which is why it is often easier to top it with fruit.

40 g/1½ oz soft vegetable margarine
75 g/3 oz wholemeal flour
1 tablespoon cornflour
3 free-range eggs
2 tablespoons clear honey
1 tablespoon boiling water
225 g/8 oz black grapes
1 medium banana
juice of ½ lemon

Lightly grease and line the base of a 20-cm/8-in cake tin. Melt the margarine over a low heat and allow to cool. Mix together the flour and cornflour. Whisk together the eggs and honey in an electric food mixer until thick and creamy then, using a metal tablespoon, fold in the margarine and water. Add the flour and, working quickly, fold in thoroughly. Pour into the tin and place in the middle of a moderately hot oven (190 c, 375 f, gas 5) and bake for 20–25 minutes until firm, springy to the touch and golden. Remove the cake from the oven and allow to cool on a wire rack. When completely cold decorate the top with the fruit.

To prepare the fruit: wash the grapes well, halve and remove the pips. Peel the banana and slice very thinly into the lemon juice. Decorate the top of the gâteau with a circle of grapes on the outside followed by banana inside that circle. **Serves 8**

Honey Yogurt Gâteau

ILLUSTRATED ON PAGES 106–7
140 calories per serving

The yogurt topping on this cake turns into a lovely creamy, thick mixture making a natural frosting to the cake. The honey used in the cake and topping can be a strongly flavoured variety because it is the taste of the honey, contrasting with the yogurt that makes it special.

3 free-range eggs
75 g/3 oz clear honey, such as Spanish Orange blossom or Hymettus
2 drops natural vanilla essence
100 g/4 oz wholemeal flour
150 ml/¼ pint natural yogurt
2 teaspoons honey
natural yogurt for serving

Lightly grease and line the base of a 20-cm/8-in cake tin. Whisk together the eggs and honey until thick and ropey. Add the vanilla essence and the wholemeal flour, folding in with a metal tablespoon. Pour into the prepared cake tin and bake in a moderately hot oven (200 c, 400 f, gas 6) for 15 minutes until firm, springy to the touch and golden brown. Remove from the oven and, when cool enough to handle, remove from the tin and place on a wire cooling rack.

While still warm spread the yogurt over the top of the cake and drizzle over the honey. Leave until cold. Make at least 3 hours before serving because the yogurt topping improves with about half a day's keeping. Serve at room temperature or chilled. Offer more yogurt separately as required. **Serves 6**

Overleaf: *Peach Roulade (page 108), Honey Yogurt Gâteau (page 105), Hazelnut Roulade (page 109), Individual Orange Torten (page 110)*

Peach Roulade

ILLUSTRATED ON PAGES 106–7

105 calories per serving

This is, I think, a very exciting and original roulade that combines a creamy but light fresh peach filling with a featherlight sponge.

3 free-range eggs
2 tablespoons clear honey
75 g/3 oz wholemeal flour
2 peaches
100 g/4 oz strained Greek yogurt
15 g/½ oz powdered gelatine
4 tablespoons orange juice
peach slices to decorate (optional)

Line a Swiss-roll tin with greaseproof paper. Whisk the eggs and honey together until thick and creamy. Using a metal tablespoon, fold the flour into the mixture. Pour into the prepared tin and level the surface. Bake in a moderately hot oven (190 c, 375 f, gas 5) for 15 minutes, until firm and springy to the touch. Remove from the oven and invert onto a clean piece of greaseproof paper. Peel off the paper in which the roll was cooked, trim the edges and roll up. Leave on a wire cooling rack.

While the sponge is cooking prepare the filling. Pour boiling water onto the peaches and then plunge into cold water. The skins should now be easy to peel off. If the peaches are very ripe they can be easily peeled without plunging in boiling water. Roughly chop one of the peaches and place it in a liquidiser with the yogurt and blend to a purée. Sprinkle the gelatine onto the orange juice in a small basin over a saucepan of hot water and stir to dissolve, then cool. Chop the remaining peach and when the gelatine is on the point of setting stir into the peach purée with the chopped peach. Carefully unroll the cooled roulade and spread with the peach mixture. Re-roll and keep chilled until required. Decorate with slices of peach along the top if you like. **Serves 8**

Hazelnut Roulade

ILLUSTRATED ON PAGES 106–7

150 calories per serving

This is wonderfully light and has a superb nutty flavour and aroma which contrasts well with the thick, creamy Greek yogurt filling. It is also very good served with Blackberry and Apple Sauce (see page 112).

3 free-range eggs
3 tablespoons clear honey
2 teaspoons hazelnut oil
1 tablespoon boiling water
50 g/2 oz ground hazelnuts
50 g/2 oz wholemeal flour
225 g/8 oz strained Greek yogurt
about 75 g/3 oz chopped hazelnuts to decorate (optional)

Line a Swiss-roll tin with non-stick baking parchment. Whisk together the eggs and honey until thick and creamy. Add the hazelnut oil and water and fold in the hazelnuts and flour, using a metal tablespoon. Work quickly to retain as much air as possible in the mixture, but ensure that all the flour is well combined. Pour onto the prepared tin, tipping to get an even spread of mixture. Bake in a moderate oven (180 c, 350 F, gas 4) for 12 minutes, until light and springy to the touch. While the roulade is baking, place a sheet of greaseproof paper on a flat work surface and dampen a clean tea-towel. When baked remove the roulade from the oven and turn out onto the paper. Cover with the damp tea-towel and, when cool enough to handle, peel off the paper and trim the edges of the roulade with a sharp knife. Roll up at once with the greaseproof paper inside. Leave to cool on a wire rack. Before serving carefully unroll and, using a palette knife, spread the yogurt over the roulade. Re-roll, cover with chopped hazelnuts if desired and serve.
Serves 8

Individual Orange Torten

ILLUSTRATED ON PAGES 106–7

120 calories per serving

Making individual desserts is not only more attractive in many cases than larger dishes but it also avoids second helpings and over-eating!

1 orange
1½ tablespoons no-added sugar apricot jam or marmalade
3 free-range eggs, separated
3 level tablespoons clear honey
juice and zest of 1 orange
drop of natural orange oil essence
75 g/3 oz wholemeal flour

Lightly grease six darioles or individual cake tins of about 7.5-cm/3-in. in diameter and 5-cm/2-in depth.

Peel the orange, removing all the pith, and reserving a small amount of rind. Slice this orange into six rounds, removing the pips. Blanch the piece of rind in boiling water then cut into very thin, small pieces, mix these with the jam and spread on top of the orange slices. Place the slices into the moulds, jam sides down.

Using an electric mixer, whisk the egg yolks and honey until thick and creamy. Add the orange juice and zest and the essence. Fold in the flour using a metal tablespoon. Whisk half the egg whites until stiff and fold into the mixture. (The remaining egg white can be kept in the refrigerator and used for another recipe.) Pour into the prepared tins and bake in a moderate oven (180 c, 350 f, gas 4) for 20 minutes until risen, golden brown and firm but springy to the touch. Serve hot or cold. **Makes 6**

Sauces and Creams

Orange Foam Sauce

ILLUSTRATED ON PAGE 115
100 calories per serving

grated rind and juice of 1 large orange
extra orange juice, if necessary
25 g/1 oz unsalted butter
2 teaspoons wholemeal flour
2 teaspoons fructose
1 free-range egg, separated
3 teaspoons lemon juice

Grate the rind from the orange and squeeze the juice, making the quantity of liquid up to 150 ml/¼ pint with the extra orange juice. Place the juice and rind in a liquidiser with the butter, flour, fructose and egg yolk. Blend to a smooth purée and pour into a heavy-based saucepan. Stir over a low heat until the mixture thickens, continue cooking over a low heat for 2 minutes to cook the flour. Remove from the heat and cover. Stand for 5 minutes. Whisk the egg white until stiff and just before serving fold into the sauce, together with the lemon juice.
Serves 4 in small portions

Orange Sauce

150 calories in total

3 oranges
2 tablespoons no-added sugar marmalade or apricot jam
1 teaspoon potato flour mixed with 2 tablespoons cold water

Roughly chop the flesh of 2 oranges and place in a saucepan with the grated rind and juice of the third orange. Stir in the marmalade or jam and cook over a low heat for 15 minutes. Liquidise the mixture, sieve and return to the saucepan. Add the potato flour and return to the heat, stirring all the time until the sauce has thickened. Pour into a jug and serve hot. This sauce may also be cooled, chilled and stored in the refrigerator in a clean, screw top (non-metallic) jar and used cold. **Serves 3–4**

Blackberry and Apple Sauce

ILLUSTRATED ON PAGES 78–9
220 calories in total

1 large cooking apple
juice of $\frac{1}{2}$ lemon
225 g/8 oz blackberries
150 ml/$\frac{1}{4}$ pint water
1 tablespoon clear honey
1 teaspoon arrowroot or potato flour mixed with 2 tablespoons cold water (optional)

Peel, slice and core the apple and toss immediately in the lemon juice to prevent browning and oxidation. Place in a saucepan with the washed blackberries and the water and cook over a gentle heat for 15 minutes. Cool slightly and pour into a liquidiser and purée with the honey. Press through a sieve and use immediately, or cool. For a thicker sauce place in a saucepan with the arrowroot or potato flour mixture and, stirring all the time over a low heat, allow to thicken. **Makes about 300 ml/$\frac{1}{2}$ pint**

Raspberry Sauce

ILLUSTRATED ON PAGES 23, 34–5 AND 78–9

90 calories per serving

Grenadine seems to enhance the natural flavour of the raspberries. It is a syrup imported from France and available in some off licences, delicatessens and supermarkets. Sirop de grenadine is made without colouring and artificial additives; it contains sugar, vanilla, citric acid and natural colouring from the pomegrantes from which it is made.

175 g/6 oz fresh raspberries
1 tablespoon grenadine
½ teaspoon potato flour mixed with 1 tablespoon cold water

Wash the raspberries and liquidise them, then sieve into a saucepan. Add the grenadine and potato flour and stir over a medium heat until the sauce thickens. Use hot or cold. **Serves 4**

Coffee Sauce

55 calories per serving

I like coffee sauce with fresh pineapple. The flavours are at their best if both the pineapple and the sauce are either at room temperature or chilled – don't serve the pineapple straight from the refrigerator with a warm sauce.

150 ml/¼ pint skimmed milk
150 ml/¼ pint strong, fresh, decaffeinated coffee
15 g/½ oz raw cane sugar
1 free-range egg
2 teaspoons Tia Maria (optional)

Mix together the milk and coffee and warm in a saucepan. Whisk together the sugar and egg in a food processor or mixer and pour the warm coffee and milk. Whisk again. Return to a clean saucepan and stir carefully over a moderate heat until the sauce thickens. Do not allow to boil or the sauce will curdle. Stir in the Tia Maria, if used, and serve hot or cold.

Cherry Sauce

45 calories per serving

This is a thick, creamy sauce that is best served chilled.

175 g/6 oz ripe, juicy dark cherries
8 tablespoons cold water
2 tablespoons redcurrant juice
2 generous tablespoons strained Greek yogurt

Wash the cherries, remove the stalks and stone. Place in a saucepan with the cold water and cook over a low heat for 20 minutes. Keep the lid on the saucepan to reserve moisture and add a little more water if necessary to prevent burning. Place in a liquidiser with the redcurrant juice and blend to a purée. Remove to a mixing bowl and allow to cool completely before stirring in the yogurt. Chill before use. **Serves 4 in small portions**

Victoria Plum Sauce

ILLUSTRATED ON PAGES 78–9

60 calories per serving

The fruit is not peeled for this sauce which helps give it a beautiful deep salmon pinkish colour. Use other yellowish plums if Victoria are not available. I rarely add sugar to fruit, but the tartness of the plums is accentuated in the sauce and even though you might not add sugar when usually cooking plums the sauce does benefit from a little.

175 g/6 oz Victoria plums
8 tablespoons cold water
50 g/2 oz fructose

Wash the plums and quarter them, removing the stones. Place in a saucepan over a low heat with the water and cover. Simmer for 10 minutes. Remove from the heat and stir in the fructose. Cool slightly before liquidising. **Serves 4 in small portions**

Tofu Cream and Passion Fruit Curd Cake (pages 118 & 81), Fruit Yogurt (page 121), Orange Foam Sauce and Wholewheat Pancakes (page 111 & 85)

Peach and Raspberry Sauce

ILLUSTRATED ON PAGE 90

35 calories per serving

175 g/6 oz raspberries
2 peaches

Wash the raspberries and place them in a liquidiser. Place the peaches in a bowl of boiling water for 2 minutes. Drain and plunge into cold water. The skins should now slip off easily. Stone the peaches and roughly chop the flesh into the liquidiser. Add the raspberries and blend to a smooth purée. Sieve before serving. **Serves 4**

Tofu Strawberry Cream

250 calories in total

This is a nice thick cream with a good flavour that can be used to fill

choux balls and puffs as well as gâteaux.

225 g/8 oz strawberries
225 g/8 oz tofu
1 tablespoon grenadine
2 teaspoons arrowroot mixed with 1 tablespoon cold water

Wash and hull the strawberries and place in a liquidiser with the tofu. Blend to a smooth purée and pour into a saucepan. Place over a moderate heat and bring to simmering point. Remove from the heat and stir in the grenadine and arrowroot. Return to the heat, still stirring, and continue cooking until the mixture is very thick. Pour into a basin and allow to cool before chilling in the refrigerator. If a smoother consistency is required return to the liquidiser and blend again for a few seconds before use. **Makes about 450 g/1 lb**

Confectioner's Custard

ILLUSTRATED ON PAGE 90
540 calories in total

This is used to fill choux buns and Paris-Brest rings, gâteaux and tarts and is traditionally made from lots of eggs, sugar and double cream. Today it is more likely that the baker is using a cheap, artificial substitute created by food technologists that just needs water adding. Either way you are better off with this new, low-calorie version! Less rich (and cheaper versions) are sometimes made with sugar, eggs, milk, flour and butter. In this version skimmed milk is used and the number of eggs and amount of sugar has been drastically reduced.

3 free-range egg yolks
50 g/2 oz fructose
1 teaspoon natural vanilla essence
450 ml/¾ pint skimmed milk
15 g/½ oz powdered gelatine
4 tablespoons boiling water

Whisk together the egg yolks, fructose, vanilla essence and milk then place in a saucepan over a moderate heat. Stir all the time until the mixture thickens but be careful not to let it boil or it will curdle. Alternatively the milk mixture could be placed in the top of a double boiler (or in a basin standing in a saucepan of hot water) and cooked in this way. Remove from the heat when it has thickened and pour into a basin to cool.

Dissolve the gelatine by sprinkling onto the boiling water in a small basin and stirring until dissolved. If it does not dissolve stand the basin in a saucepan of hot water until it does. Remove from the heat and allow to cool. When on point of setting fold the gelatine into the custard. Leave to cool slightly. Whisk the egg whites until stiff and fold into the custard. Leave to set in the refrigerator before use for about 1 hour. If the mixture sets more firmly than is required blend in a liquidiser until it has reached the required consistency. **Makes about 600 ml/1 pint**

Tofu Cream

ILLUSTRATED ON PAGE 115
420 calories in total

This can be used in the same way as Confectioner's Custard. It is completely free from dairy produce and is set using agar-agar (a vegetable setting agent) so it is useful for vegetarians and vegans.

3 tablespoons concentrated apple juice
7 tablespoons cold water
175 g/6 oz tofu
50 g/2 oz tahini
½ teaspoon agar-agar soaked in 4 tablespoons cold water

Mix together the apple juice and water then place, together with the tofu and tahini, in a saucepan. Separately place the agar-agar in a saucepan and bring to the boil to dissolve the setting agent. Allow to cool. Heat the tofu mixture, which should be thick and creamy, and remove from the heat. Stir in the agar-agar, mixing thoroughly, then pour the mixture into a basin to cool. **Makes a good 300 ml/½ pint**

Chantilly Cream

300 calories in total

This is a healthy version of the classic French cream often used with choux pastry. Instead of double cream and icing sugar it uses thick, strained Greek yogurt flavoured with vanilla essence.

225 g/8 oz strained Greek yogurt
1 free-range egg white
2 drops natural vanilla essence

Place the yogurt in a mixing bowl. Whisk the egg white until stiff. Stir the vanilla essence into the yogurt. Lighten the mixture by mixing in 2 tablespoons whisked egg white, then fold in the remainder. This cream is best chilled, so make sure all the ingredients are cold before you start. **Makes 300 ml/½ pint**

Carob Cream

300 calories in total

Carob is used in place of cocoa or chocolate because it does not contain caffeine, theobromine and oxalic acid (see main glossary). It has a chocolate flavour and is available as a powder or in bars. Here we use the bars to make a cream that can be used in the same way as confectioner's custard. This mixture sets like a blancmange but just before use it should be whisked in a liquidiser to return it to a creamy consistency which it will then retain.

25 g/1 oz skimmed milk powder
250 ml/8 fl oz cold water
1 (42-g/1½-oz) bar plain carob
2 drops natural vanilla essence
¼-½ teaspoon agar-agar dissolved in 4 tablespoons cold water

Sprinkle the skimmed milk powder onto the water and place in a saucepan over a moderate heat. Break up the carob bar and place in the top of a double boiler or in a basin standing in a saucepan of hot water to melt the carob. While it is melting pour a little hot milk on to the carob, stirring all the time, gradually adding a little more milk until the mixture can be easily poured into the milk pan. Add the vanilla essence to the mixture. Continue stirring until the milk and carob are well mixed. Remove from the heat. Place the agar-agar in a saucepan and bring to the boil to dissolve. Remove from the heat and allow to cool, then stir into the carob mixture. Pour through a sieve into a basin and allow to cool and set. Refrigerate.

Just before use place in liquidiser and blend to creamy consistency.
Makes 300 ml/½ pint

Variation: Light Carob Cream is made in the same way as the above recipe but fold 2 whisked free-range egg whites into the mixture after it has cooled but not set.

Yogurts and Custards

Natural Yogurt

233 calories

600 ml/1 pint skimmed milk
1 tablespoon natural live yogurt
1 tablespoon skimmed milk powder

Place the milk in a saucepan and heat to 50 c/100 f. Mix together the yogurt and milk powder to make a smooth paste. Pour the warm milk onto the paste and stir well. Place the mixture in a vacuum jug and seal. Alternatively place in an electric, or other type of, yogurt maker. Incubate for 6–8 hours then place in the refrigerator to chill thoroughly before using.

Previous batches of home-made yogurt or bought natural yogurt can be used as starters. Most purchased yogurts are live even if they do not state the word 'live' on the packaging. The bacteria needed to make yogurt (i.e. ferment the lactose or milk sugar into lactic acid) will be killed by extreme heat such as UHT (long-life) treatment so long-life yogurts are not suitable for making your own yogurt. Most yogurts are made from pasteurised milk, and this does not effect the bacteria because they are added after-pateurisation.

If using goats' milk instead of cows' milk to make your yogurt then choose a natural goats' milk yogurt as a starter. Do not make your yogurt from starters of fruit yogurts, this is because such yogurts often contain additives such as sugar, colouring, preservatives, stabilisers, modified starches etc. Fruit also introduces other micro-organisms into the

yogurt which may interfere with the process of fermentation by the bacteria, and it will alter the acidity of the yogurt – you might end up with some very odd flavoured yogurts! There are also yeasts in fruit that it would not be a good idea to incubate during yogurt making. **Makes 600 ml/1 pint**

Fruit Yogurt

ILLUSTRATED ON PAGES 23 AND 115

After making and chilling your natural yogurt you can flavour it with any fruit of your choice. But remember it is best to add the fruit shortly before using because you are introducing spoilage micro-organisms with the fruit. This is nothing to worry about, but it does mean that the yogurt may deteriorate a lot quicker than it would without the fruit. It is also best to cut your fruit shortly before use to minimise loss of nutrients such as vitamins and minerals which begin to oxidise and be destroyed as soon as the fruit is cut. Use a stainless steel knife to cut fruit.

Make any combination of fruit to your taste to mix with yogurt. If you are feeling uninspired you might try some of the following:
• yogurt with a little Greek honey drizzled over it in a serving glass is a traditional and delicious dessert
• scoop the pips and juice from a passion fruit to flavour two servings of natural yogurt
• fresh raspberries are delicious when swirled into yogurt
• lightly poached and cooled blackcurrants really give yogurt a lively, tangy kick
• freshly picked strawberries are very good, too; strawberries that are just a little over-ripe give a good juicy flavour
• mash some ripe banana with a small amount of lemon juice and make a banana yogurt purée
• muesli is good stirred into yogurt, especially one that is generous with the hazelnuts
• granola cereals (of the Original Crunchy type) are good in yogurt, but add just before serving so they stay crispy
• cooked and cooled dried fruits like prunes and apricots can be finely chopped, or puréed, and stirred into yogurt
• fresh figs are wonderful with natural yogurt
• mangoes are expensive, but if you are making something with a mango reserve a few teaspoonfuls of pulp and stir it into your natural yogurt.

Strained Yogurt

To make strained yogurt you simply place the yogurt in some butter muslin or cheesecloth and suspend it over a draining board or tray to allow all the whey to drain out of the yogurt. This can be done overnight in a warmish room and the result is a thick, creamy yogurt which does not separate into curds and whey as does ordinary yogurt. It is very useful for healthy desserts and makes an excellent substitute for heavy creams.

Strained Greek yogurt is now readily available in many health food shops, wholefood shops, delicatessens and supermarkets. It is very delicious and silky smooth, but it lacks that tang found in natural yogurts which have not been strained. This makes them better for more savoury dishes and for marinades and sauces.

Coffee Pots

45 calories per serving

2 teaspoons demerara sugar
1 tablespoon skimmed milk powder
300 ml/$\frac{1}{2}$ pint hot decaffeinated coffee
2 free-range eggs
25 g/1 oz toasted hazelnuts, finely chopped

Place four small ramekins in a roasting tin and fill the tin with sufficient boiling water to come two-thirds of the way up the sides of the ramekins, thus creating a bain-marie.

Dissolve the sugar and milk powder in the coffee and leave to cool. Whisk the eggs until frothy then add the coffee mixture. Stir in the hazelnuts and pour the mixture into the ramekins. Bake in a moderate oven (180 c, 350 f, gas 4) for 45–50 minutes. Allow to cool and chill before serving. **Makes 4**

Indian Mango Milk Pudding

85 calories per serving

This is a deliciously thick and creamy dessert which is very low in calories and hardly deserves the title 'milk pudding' because it is so much more exciting in colour and flavour. I like this dessert at room temperature, but most people prefer it chilled.

600 ml/1 pint skimmed milk
pinch of saffron strands
5 green cardamoms
1 large ripe mango
2 free-range eggs
300 ml/½ pint thick-set natural yogurt

Butter a shallow 900-ml/1½-pint pie dish. Place the milk, saffron strands and cardamoms in a saucepan over a low heat and bring to just below boiling point. Remove from the heat, cover and leave to infuse for 15 minutes. Peel the mango and cut into thin slices, arrange them in the base of the dish. Beat the eggs and yogurt together in a bowl. Pour the milk through a sieve into a jug (to catch the saffron and cardamoms) and then pour onto the egg-yogurt mixture, stirring all the time to prevent it going lumpy. Pour onto the mango and set the pie dish in a roasting tin containing 2.5-cm/1-in boiling water. Bake in a moderate oven (180 c, 350 f, gas 4) for 35 minutes until golden and set. Cool and chill before serving. **Serves 6**

Index